CHINA IN THE 21ST CENTURY

CHINA AND THE U.S.

TRADE AND COMMITMENT ISSUES

CHINA IN THE 21ST CENTURY

Additional books in this series can be found on Nova's website
under the Series tab.

Additional e-books in this series can be found on Nova's website
under the e-book tab.

CHINA IN THE 21ST CENTURY

CHINA AND THE U.S.

TRADE AND COMMITMENT ISSUES

ARTHUR SANTONI
EDITOR

New York

Copyright © 2014 by Nova Science Publishers, Inc.

All rights reserved. No part of this book may be reproduced, stored in a retrieval system or transmitted in any form or by any means: electronic, electrostatic, magnetic, tape, mechanical photocopying, recording or otherwise without the written permission of the Publisher.

For permission to use material from this book please contact us:
Telephone 631-231-7269; Fax 631-231-8175
Web Site: http://www.novapublishers.com

NOTICE TO THE READER

The Publisher has taken reasonable care in the preparation of this book, but makes no expressed or implied warranty of any kind and assumes no responsibility for any errors or omissions. No liability is assumed for incidental or consequential damages in connection with or arising out of information contained in this book. The Publisher shall not be liable for any special, consequential, or exemplary damages resulting, in whole or in part, from the readers' use of, or reliance upon, this material. Any parts of this book based on government reports are so indicated and copyright is claimed for those parts to the extent applicable to compilations of such works.

Independent verification should be sought for any data, advice or recommendations contained in this book. In addition, no responsibility is assumed by the publisher for any injury and/or damage to persons or property arising from any methods, products, instructions, ideas or otherwise contained in this publication.

This publication is designed to provide accurate and authoritative information with regard to the subject matter covered herein. It is sold with the clear understanding that the Publisher is not engaged in rendering legal or any other professional services. If legal or any other expert assistance is required, the services of a competent person should be sought. FROM A DECLARATION OF PARTICIPANTS JOINTLY ADOPTED BY A COMMITTEE OF THE AMERICAN BAR ASSOCIATION AND A COMMITTEE OF PUBLISHERS.

Additional color graphics may be available in the e-book version of this book.

Library of Congress Cataloging-in-Publication Data

ISBN: 978-1-63321-156-8

Published by Nova Science Publishers, Inc. † New York

CONTENTS

Preface		vii
Chapter 1	China-U.S. Trade Issues *Wayne M. Morrison*	1
Chapter 2	U.S.-China Trade: United States Has Secured Commitments in Key Bilateral Dialogues, but U.S. Agency Reporting on Status Should be Improved *United States Government Accountability Office*	71
Chapter 3	24th U.S. - China Joint Commission on Commerce and Trade Fact Sheet *United States Department of Commerce*	113
Chapter 4	U.S. Fact Sheet: Economic Track Fifth Meeting of the U.S.-China Strategic and Economic Dialogue *United States Department of the Treasury*	119
Index		125

PREFACE

Economic and trade reforms begun in 1979 have helped transform China into one of the world's fastest-growing economies. China's economic growth and trade liberalization, including comprehensive trade commitments made upon entering the World Trade Organization (WTO) in 2001, have led to a sharp expansion in U.S.-China commercial ties. Yet, bilateral trade relations have become increasingly strained in recent years over a number of issues, including a large and growing U.S. trade deficit with China, resistance by China to appreciate its currency to market levels, China's mixed record on implementing its WTO obligations, infringement of U.S. intellectual property (including through cyber espionage), and numerous Chinese industrial policies that appear to impose new restrictions on foreign firms or provide unfair advantages to domestic Chinese firms (such as subsidies). This book provides an overview of U.S.-China commercial relations, including major trade disputes.

Chapter 1 – U.S.-China economic ties have expanded substantially over the past three decades. Total U.S.-China trade rose from $2 billion in 1979 to $562 billion in 2013. China is currently the United States' second-largest trading partner, its third-largest export market, and its biggest source of imports. China is estimated to be a $300 billion market for U.S. firms (based on U.S. exports to China and sales by U.S.-invested firms in China). Many U.S. firms view participation in China's market as critical to staying globally competitive. General Motors (GM), for example, which has invested heavily in China, sold more cars in China than in the United States each year from 2010 to 2013. In addition, U.S. imports of low-cost goods from China greatly benefit U.S. consumers, and U.S. firms that use China as the final point of assembly for their products, or use Chinese-made inputs for production in the

United States, are able to lower costs. China is the largest foreign holder of U.S. Treasury securities ($1.3 trillion as of November 2013). China's purchases of U.S. government debt help keep U.S. interest rates low.

Chapter 2 – China is the largest destination for U.S. exports outside North America and also the source of the largest U.S. bilateral trade deficit. The countries engage in two high-level dialogues to address trade barriers and cross- cutting economic issues. These are the JCCT, co-led for the United States by Commerce and USTR, and the economic track of the S&ED, led by Treasury. GAO was asked to review China's bilateral trade commitments made in these dialogues. This report (1) describes trade and investment commitments China has made at the JCCT and S&ED; (2) describes U.S. agency tracking of China's implementation of these commitments; and (3) evaluates U.S. agency reporting on implementation. GAO analyzed documents, including public fact sheets stating commitments; interviewed officials, industry representatives, and other experts; used a structured process to categorize commitments; and reviewed reports officials identified as reporting implementation status of commitments.

Chapter 3 – U.S. Commerce Secretary Penny Pritzker and U.S. Trade Representative Michael Froman, together with Chinese Vice Premier Wang Yang, co-chaired the 24th U.S.-China Joint Commission on Commerce and Trade (JCCT) in Beijing, China on December 19th – 20th, 2013. They were joined by U.S. Secretary of Agriculture Tom Vilsack to address agricultural concerns. Other participants included U.S. Ambassador to China Gary Locke, U.S. Trade and Development Agency Director Leocadia Zak, and representatives from the State and Treasury Departments.

Chapter 4 – Report of U.S. Fact Sheet – Economic Track Fifth Meeting of the U.S.-China Strategic and Economic Dialogue, dated July 12, 2013.

In: China and the U.S.
Editor: Arthur Santoni

ISBN: 978-1-63321-156-8
© 2014 Nova Science Publishers, Inc.

Chapter 1

CHINA-U.S. TRADE ISSUES[*]

Wayne M. Morrison

SUMMARY

U.S.-China economic ties have expanded substantially over the past three decades. Total U.S.-China trade rose from $2 billion in 1979 to $562 billion in 2013. China is currently the United States' second-largest trading partner, its third-largest export market, and its biggest source of imports. China is estimated to be a $300 billion market for U.S. firms (based on U.S. exports to China and sales by U.S.-invested firms in China). Many U.S. firms view participation in China's market as critical to staying globally competitive. General Motors (GM), for example, which has invested heavily in China, sold more cars in China than in the United States each year from 2010 to 2013. In addition, U.S. imports of low-cost goods from China greatly benefit U.S. consumers, and U.S. firms that use China as the final point of assembly for their products, or use Chinese-made inputs for production in the United States, are able to lower costs. China is the largest foreign holder of U.S. Treasury securities ($1.3 trillion as of November 2013). China's purchases of U.S. government debt help keep U.S. interest rates low.

Despite growing commercial ties, the bilateral economic relationship has become increasingly complex and often fraught with tension. From the U.S.

---

[*] This is an edited, reformatted and augmented version of a Congressional Research Service publication, CRS Report for Congress, RL33536, dated February 10, 2014.

perspective, many trade tensions stem from China's incomplete transition to a free market economy. While China has significantly liberalized its economic and trade regimes over the past three decades, it continues to maintain (or has recently imposed) a number of state-directed policies that appear to distort trade and investment flows. Major areas of concern expressed by U.S. policy makers and stakeholders include China's relatively poor record of intellectual property rights (IPR) enforcement and alleged widespread cyber espionage against U.S. firms by Chinese government entities; its mixed record on implementing its World Trade Organization (WTO) obligations; its extensive use of industrial policies (such as financial support of state-owned firms, trade and investment barriers, and pressure on foreign-invested firms in China to transfer technology in exchange for market access) in order to promote the development of industries favored by the government and protect them from foreign competition; and its policies to maintain an undervalued currency. Many U.S. policy makers argue that such policies harm U.S. economic interests and have contributed to U.S. job losses. For example, one study estimated that Chinese IPR infringement cost the U.S. economy up to $240 billion annually. There are a number of views in the United States over how to more effectively address commercial disputes with China:

- Take a more aggressive stand against China, such as increasing the number of dispute settlement cases brought against China in the WTO, or threatening to impose trade sanctions against China unless it addresses policies (such as IPR theft) that hurt U.S. economic interests.
- Intensify negotiations through existing high-level bilateral dialogues, such as the U.S.-China Strategic & Economic Dialogue (S&ED), which was established to discuss long-term challenges in the relationship. In addition, seek to complete ongoing U.S. negotiations with China to reach a high-standard bilateral investment treaty (BIT), as well as to finalize negotiations in the WTO toward achieving China's accession to the Government Procurement Agreement (GPA).
- Encourage China to join the Trans-Pacific Partnership (TPP) negotiations and/or seek to negotiate a bilateral a free trade agreement (FTA) with China.
- Continue to press China to implement comprehensive economic reforms, such as diminishing the role of the state in the economy and implementing policies to boost domestic consumption.

Economic and trade reforms begun in 1979 have helped transform China into one of the world's fastest-growing economies. China's economic growth and trade liberalization, including comprehensive trade commitments made upon entering the World Trade Organization (WTO) in 2001, have led to a sharp expansion in U.S.-China commercial ties. Yet, bilateral trade relations have become increasingly strained in recent years over a number of issues, including a large and growing U.S. trade deficit with China, resistance by China to appreciate its currency to market levels, China's mixed record on implementing its WTO obligations, infringement of U.S. intellectual property (including through cyber espionage), and numerous Chinese industrial policies that appear to impose new restrictions on foreign firms or provide unfair advantages to domestic Chinese firms (such as subsidies). Several Members of Congress have called on the Obama Administration to take a tougher stance against China to induce it to eliminate trade and economic policies deemed harmful to U.S. economic interests and/or inconsistent with WTO rules. This report provides an overview of U.S.-China commercial relations, including major trade disputes.

MOST RECENT DEVELOPMENTS

On January 23, 2014, Lenovo, a Chinese technology company, announced that it would purchase IBM's x86 server business for $2.3 billion. On January 29, 2014, Lenovo announced that it would acquire Motorola Mobility from Google for $2.9 billion.

From November 9 to 12, 2013, the Communist Party of China held the 3rd Plenum of its 18th Party Congress, a meeting that many analysts anticipated would result in the initiation of extensive new economic reforms. Following the meeting, the Communist Party issued a communique with a number of broad policy statements. One highlighted by the Chinese media was that the market would now play a "decisive" role in allocating resources in the economy.

On September 26, 2013, the Chinese government announced that it would join negotiations in the WTO for a trade in services agreement.

On August 5, 2013, the USTR announced that the United States had largely prevailed in a WTO dispute settlement case against China over its use of high antidumping and countervailing duties on U.S. chicken broiler products.

On July 17, 2013, the USTR expressed disappointment over the suspension of WTO negotiations on reaching a new information technology agreement, stating that China's hardline position in the negotiations was largely to blame for lack of an agreement.

On July 10-11, 2013, the fifth round of talks under the U.S.-China Strategic and Economic Dialogue (S&ED) was held in Washington, DC. China announced its intention to negotiate a high-standard bilateral investment treaty with the United States that would include all stages of investment and all sectors.

On June 7-8, 2013, President Obama and Chinese President Xi Jinping held discussions on major bilateral issues. President Obama warned that if cyber security issues are not addressed and if there continues to be direct theft of United States property, then "this was going to be very difficult problem in the economic relationship and was going to be an inhibitor to the relationship really reaching its full potential."

On May 29, 2013, Shuanghui International Holdings, the majority owner of China's largest meat processing enterprise, announced it was seeking to purchase Smithfield Foods, the largest U.S. pork producer, for $7.1 billion. Although several Members of Congress expressed concern over how the acquisition would affect U.S. food safety, the deal was completed on September 26, 2013.

On March 11, 2013, Tom Donilon, National SecurityAdvisor to President Obama, stated in a speech that the United States and China should engage in a constructive dialogue to establish acceptable norms of behavior in cyberspace; that China should recognize the urgency and scope of the problem and the risks it poses to U.S. trade relations and the reputation to Chinese industry; and that China should take serious steps to investigate and stop cyber espionage.

On February 19, 2013, Mandiant, a U.S. information security company, issued a report documenting extensive economic cyber espionage by a Chinese unit with alleged links to the Chinese People's LiberationArmy (PLA) against 141 firms, covering 20 industries, since 2006.

U.S. TRADE WITH CHINA[1]

U.S.-China trade rose rapidly after the two nations reestablished diplomatic relations (in January 1979), signed a bilateral trade agreement (July 1979), and provided mutual most-favored-nation (MFN) treatment beginning in 1980.[2] In 1979 (when China's economic reforms began), total U.S.-China trade (exports plus imports) was $2 billion; China ranked as the United States' 23rd-largest export market and its 45th-largest source of imports. In 2013, total bilateral trade (exports plus imports) reached $562 billion. China is currently the second-largest U.S. trading partner (after Canada), the third-largest U.S. export market (after Canada and Mexico), and the largest source of U.S. imports. In recent years, China has been one of the fastest-growing U.S. export markets, and the importance of this market is expected to grow even further, given the pace of China's economic growth, and as Chinese living standards continue to improve and a sizable Chinese middle class emerges. According to one estimate, China is currently a $300 billion market for U.S. firms if U.S. exports to China and sales by U.S.-invested firms in China are counted.[3]

A major concern among some U.S. policy makers has been the size of the U.S. trade deficit with China. That deficit rose from $10 billion in 1990 to $266 billion in 2008; it fell to $227 billion in 2009 (due largely to the effects of the global economic downturn), then rose over each of the next three years, reaching $318 billion in 2013 (see Table 1 and Figure 1). For the past several years, the U.S. trade deficit with China has been significantly larger than that with any other U.S. trading partner and several trading groups. Some analysts contend that the large U.S. trade deficit is an indicator that the trade relationship is unbalanced, unfair, and damaging to the U.S. economy, while others argue that the large U.S. trade deficit with China is a reflection of global supply chains because a significant level of U.S. imports from China come from foreign-invested multi-national companies there, which use China as the final point of assembly for many of their products (discussed more fully later in the report). A joint study by the Organization for Economic Cooperation and Development (OECD) and the WTO estimated that the U.S trade deficit in China would be reduced by 25% (in 2009) if bilateral trade flows were measured according to the value-added that occurred in each country before it was exported.[4]

U.S. Merchandise Exports to China

U.S. merchandise exports to China in 2013 were $122 billion, up 10.3% over 2012 levels. In 2013, China was the third largest U.S. merchandise export after Canada and Mexico (see Figure 2). From 2000 to 2013, the share of total U.S. exports going to China rose from 2.1% to 7.7%. As indicated in Table 2, the top five merchandise U.S. exports to China in 2013 were oilseeds and grains; aircraft and parts; waste and scrap; motor vehicles; and navigational, measuring, electro-medical, and control instruments. As indicated in **Table 3**, from 2004 to 2013, U.S. exports to China increased by 349%, which was the fastest growth rate for U.S. exports among its top 10 export markets.

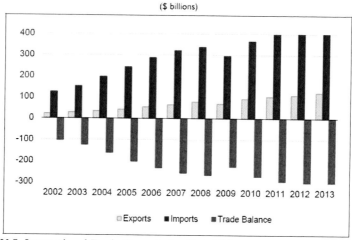

Source: U.S. International Trade Commission DataWeb.

Figure 1. U.S. Merchandise Trade with China: 2002-2013 ($ billions).

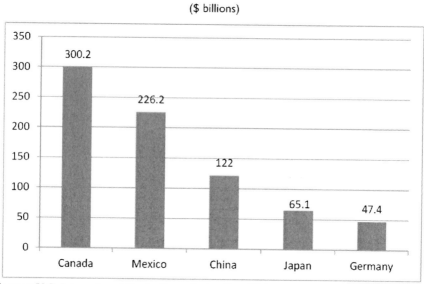

Source: U.S. International Trade Commission DataWeb.

Figure 2. Top 5 U.S. Merchandise Export Markets: 2013.

**Table 1. U.S. Merchandise Trade with China: 1980-2013
($ billions)**

Year	U.S. Exports	U.S. Imports	U.S. Trade Balance
1980	3.8	1.1	2.7
1985	3.9	3.9	0.0
1990	4.8	15.2	-10.4
1995	11.7	45.6	-33.8
2000	16.3	100.1	-83.8
2005	41.8	243.5	-201.6
2006	55.2	287.8	-232.5
2007	65.2	321.5	-256.3
2008	71.5	337.8	-266.3
2009	69.6	296.4	-226.8
2010	91.9	364.9	-273.1
2011	103.9	393.3	-295.5
2012	110.6	425.6	-315.0
2013	122.0	440.4	-318.4

Source: U.S. International Trade Commission (USITC) DataWeb.

In addition, China was the second-largest U.S. agricultural export market in 2013 at $27.9 billion. China is also a significant market for U.S. exports of private services. These totaled $30 billion in 2012, making China the fourth-largest export market for U.S. private services.[5]

Many trade analysts argue that China could prove to be a much more significant market for U.S. exports in the future. China is one of the world's fastest-growing economies, and rapid economic growth is likely to continue in the near future, provided that economic reforms are continued.[6] China's goals of modernizing its infrastructure, upgrading its industries, and improving rural living standards could generate substantial demand for foreign goods and services. Finally, economic growth has substantially improved the purchasing power of Chinese citizens, especially those living in urban areas along the east coast of China. China's growing economy, large foreign exchange reserves (at over $3.7 trillion as of September 2013), and large population of over 1.3 billion people make it a potentially enormous market. To illustrate:

Table 2. Major U.S. Exports to China: 2009-2013
($ millions and percent change)

NAIC Commodity	2009	2010	2011	2012	2013	2012-2013 % change
Total Exports to China	69,576	91,878	103,879	110,590	122,016	10.3%
Oilseeds and grains	9,376	11,208	11,500	16,546	16,092	-2.7%
Aerospace products and parts	5,344	5,766	6,392	8,367	12,620	50.8%
Waste and scrap	7,142	8,561	11,540	9,526	8,765	-8.0%
Motor vehicles	1,134	3,515	5,369	5,788	8,614	48.8%
Navigational, measuring, electro-medical, and controlling instruments	2,917	3,782	4,275	5,153	5,732	11.2%
Semiconductors and other electronic components	6,041	7,555	5,668	4,859	5,724	17.8%
Basic chemicals	3,433	4,202	4,658	4,716	4,934	4.6%
Resin, synthetic rubber, & artificial & synthetic fibers & filament	4,036	4,336	4,476	4,278	4,237	-1.0%
Other general purpose machinery	1,890	2,445	3,113	3,021	3,166	4.8%
Meat products and meat packaging products	1,438	1,319	2,020	2,409	2,759	14.5%

Source: USITC DataWeb.

Note: Top 10 U.S. exports to China in 2013 using the North American Industry Classification (NAIC) System on a 4-digit level.

**Table 3. Major U.S. Merchandise Export Markets: 2004-2013
($ billions and percent change)**

Country	2004	2012	2013	Percent Change 2012-2013	Percent Change 2004-2013
Total U.S. Exports	817	1,546	1,579	2.1%	193.3
Canada	188	292	300	2.9%	159.6%
Mexico	111	216	226	4.5%	203.6%
China	35	111	122	10.3%	**348.6%**
Japan	54	70	65	-7.0%	120.4%
Germany	31	49	47	-2.8%	151.6%
UK	36	55	47	-13.6%	130.6%
Brazil	14	44	44	0.9%	314.3%
Netherlands	24	41	43	4.9%	179.2%
Hong Kong	16	37	42	13.3%	262.5%
Korea	26	42	42	-1.8%	161.5%
France	21	31	32	3.7%	152.4%
Belgium	17	29	32	7.9%	188.2%
Singapore	20	31	31	0.5%	155.0%
Switzerland	9	26	27	3.1%	300.0%
Australia	14	31	26	-16.5%	185.7%

Source: U.S. International Trade Commission DataWeb.
Note: Ranked according to the top 10 U.S. export markets in 2013.

- According to a report by the Boston Consulting Group, in 2009, China had 148 million "middle class and affluent" consumers, defined as those whose annual household income was 60,000 RMB ($9,160) or higher, and that level is projected to rise to 415 million by 2020.[7] A May 2013 Boston Consulting Group study estimated that China had 1.3 million millionaires in 2012.[8]
- Although Chinese private consumption as a percent of GDP is much lower than that of most other major economies, the rate of growth of Chinese private consumption has been rising rapidly. For example, private consumption as a percent of GDP in China in 2012 was 36.3%, compared to 71.0% in the United States. However, the annual rate of growth in Chinese private consumption from 2001 to 2012 averaged 8.4%, while the U.S. annual average was 2.0%.[9]

- China's government has indicated that it plans to step up efforts to boost domestic spending to help lessen its dependence on exports as the major contributor to China's economic growth. In 2008, China began the implementation of a $586 billion economic stimulus package, largely focused on infrastructure projects. China's goals of developing its western regions, expanding and modernizing its infrastructure, boosting its social safety net (such as health care and pensions), modernizing and developing key industries, reducing pollution, and raising incomes of the rural poor will likely result in large-scale government spending levels. China's 12th Five-Year Plan (2011-2015) reportedly will allocate $1 trillion to infrastructure spending.[10]
- China currently has the world's largest mobile phone network and one of the fastest-growing markets, with over 1.22 billion mobile phone subscribers as of October 2013.[11]
- Boeing Corporation predicts that over the next 20 years (2013-2032), China will buy 5,580 new commercial airplanes valued at $780 billion and will be Boeing's largest commercial airplane customer outside the United States.[12]
- China replaced the United States as the world's largest Internet user in 2008. At the end of June 2012, China had an estimated 538 million users versus 245 million in the United States. Yet, the percentage of the Chinese population using the Internet is small relative to the United States: 40.1% versus 78.1%, respectively.[13]
- In 2009, China became the world's largest producer of motor vehicles as well as the largest market for new vehicles.
- General Motors (GM) sold more cars and trucks in China than in the United States each year from 2010 to 2013.[14]

Major U.S. Imports from China

China was the largest source of U.S. merchandise imports in 2013, at $440 billion, up 3.5% over the previous year. China's share of total U.S. imports rose from 8.2% in 2000 to 19.1% in 2010, dropped to 18.1% in 2011, but rose to 18.7% in 2012 and to 19.4% in 2013. The importance (ranking) of China as a source of U.S. imports has risen sharply, from eighth largest in 1990, to fourth in 2000, to second in 2004-2006, to first in 2007-2013. The top five U.S. imports from China in 2011 were computer equipment, communications equipment, miscellaneous manufactured products (such as toys and games), apparel, and semiconductors and other electronic parts (see Table 4). China was also the third-largest source of U.S. agricultural imports at $4.6 billion. China was the 10th-largest source of U.S. imports of private services at $13.0 billion in 2012.[15]

Table 4. Major U.S. Merchandise Imports From China: 2009-2013
($ millions and percent change)

NAIC Commodity	2009	2010	2011	2012	2013	Percent Change 2012 - 2013
Total imports from China	296,402	364,944	399,335	425,644	440,434	3.5%
Computer equipment	44,818	59,800	68,276	68,815	68,123	-0.1%
Communications equipment	26,362	33,464	39,806	51,857	58,839	13.5%
Miscellaneous manufactured commodities	30,668	34,168	32,672	32,644	32,440	-0.6%
Apparel	22,669	26,603	27,554	26,926	27,410	1.8%
Semiconductors and other electronic components	12,363	18,263	19,835	19,012	19,363	1.8%
Footwear	13,119	15,673	16,482	16,870	16,761	-0.6%
Audio and video equipment	18,253	19,493	15,853	15,894	13,830	-13.0%
Household and institutional furniture and kitchen cabinets	9,128	11,123	11,398	12,235	13,225	8.1%
Household appliances and miscellaneous machines	7,724	9,090	9,569	10,298	11,670	13.3%
Motor vehicle parts	4,710	6,966	8,277	9,447	10,441	10.5%

Source: U.S. International Trade Commission DataWeb.
Notes: Top 10 U.S. imports from China in 2013 using the North American Industry Classification (NAIC) System on a 4-digit level.

Throughout the 1980s and 1990s, nearly all U.S. imports from China were low-value, labor-intensive products, such as toys and games, consumer electronic products, footwear, and textiles and apparel. However, over the past few years, an increasing proportion of U.S. imports from China have been comprised of more technologically advanced products (see **text box** below).

> ### U.S.-CHINA TRADE IN ADVANCED TECHNOLOGY PRODUCTS
>
> According to the U.S. Census Bureau, U.S. imports of "advanced technology products" (ATP) from China in 2013 totaled $145.9 billion. ATP products accounted for 33.1% of total U.S. imports from China, compared with 19.2% ($29.3 billion) in 2003. In addition, ATP imports from China accounted for 36.4% of total U.S ATP imports (compared with 14.1% in 2003). U.S. ATP exports to China in 2013 were $29.1 billion; these accounted for 23.9% of total U.S. exports to China and 9.1% of U.S. global ATP exports. In comparison, U.S. ATP exports to China in 2003 were $8.3 billion, which accounted for 29.2% of U.S. exports to China and 4.6% of total U.S. ATP exports.
>
> The United States ran a $116.8 billion deficit in its ATP trade with China in 2013, up from a $21.0 billion deficit in 2003. Some see the large and growing U.S. trade deficit in ATP with China as a source of concern, contending that it signifies the growing international competitiveness of China in high technology. Others dispute this, noting that a large share of the ATP imports from China are in fact relatively low-end technology products and parts, such as notebook computers, or are products that are assembled in China using imported high technology parts that are largely developed and/or made elsewhere.

China as a Major Center for Global Supply Chains

Many analysts contend that the sharp increase in U.S. imports from China (and hence the growing bilateral trade imbalance) is largely the result of movement in production facilities from other (primarily Asian) countries to

China. That is, various products that used to be made in such places as Japan, Taiwan, Hong Kong, etc., and then exported to the United States, are now being made in China (in many cases, by foreign firms in China). To illustrate, in 1990, 47.1% of the value of U.S. manufactured imports came from Pacific Rim countries (including China); this figure declined to 46.2% in 2013.[16] Over this period, the share of total U.S. manufactured imports that came from China increased rose from 3.6% to 25.9%. In other words, while China was becoming an increasingly important source for U.S. manufactured imports, the relative importance of the rest of the Pacific Rim (excluding China) as a source of U.S. imports was declining, in part because many multinational firms were shifting their export-oriented manufacturing facilities to China (see **Figure 3**). In 1990, China accounted for 7.7% of U.S. manufactured imports from all Pacific Rim countries, but by 2013, this figure grew to 55.9%.

Another illustration of the shift in production can be seen in the case of U.S. computer equipment imports, which constitute the largest category of U.S. imports from China (on an NAIC basis, 4-digit level). In 2000, Japan was the largest foreign supplier of U.S. computer equipment (with a 19.6% share of total U.S. imports), while China ranked fourth (with a 12.1% share). By 2013, Japan's ranking had fallen to fourth; the value of its shipments dropped by 70.2% over 2000 levels, and its share of U.S. computer imports declined to 3.8% (2013). China was by far the largest foreign supplier of computer equipment in 2013 with a 64.0% share of total U.S. computer equipment imports, compared to 12.0% in 2000 (see Figure 4). While U.S. imports of computer equipment from China from 2000 to 2013 rose by 725.1%, the total value of U.S. computer imports worldwide rose by only 55.1%.[17] A study by the U.S. International Trade Commission (USITC) estimated that in 2002 over 99% of computer exports in China were from foreign-invested firms in China.[18] Taiwan, one of the world's leaders in sales of information technology, produces over 90% of its information hardware equipment (such as computers) in China. Computer equipment, like many other globally traded products, often involves many stages of production, using parts and other inputs made by numerous multinational firms throughout the world, a significant share of which is assembled in China. The globalization of supply chains makes it increasingly difficult to interpret conventional U.S. trade statistics (see **text box** below).

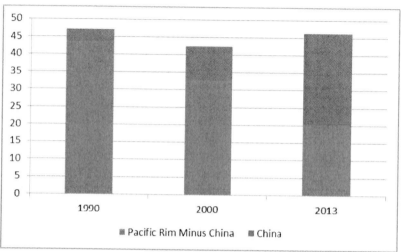

Source: U.S. International Trade Commission DataWeb.
Notes: Standard International Trade Classification (SITC) definition of manufactured imports.

Figure 3. U.S. Manufactured Imports from Pacific Rim Countries as a Percent of Total U.S. Manufactured Imports: 1990, 2000, and 2013.

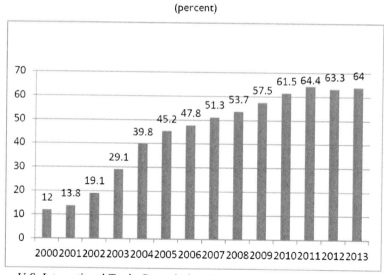

Source: U.S. International Trade Commission DataWeb.

Figure 4. U.S. Computer Imports from China as a Percentage of Total U.S. Computer Imports: 2000-2013.

GLOBAL SUPPLY CHAINS, CHINA, AND THE APPLE iPOD: WHO BENEFITS?

Many U.S. companies sign contracts with Taiwanese firms to have their products manufactured (mainly in China), and then shipped to the United States where they are sold by U.S. firms under their own brand name. In many instances, the level of value-added that occurs in China (often it simply involves assemblage) can be quite small relative to the overall cost/price of the final product. One study by researchers at the University of California looked at the production of a 2005 Apple 30 gigabyte video iPod, which is made in China by Foxconn, a Taiwanese company, using parts produced globally (mainly in Asia). The study estimated that it cost about $144 to make each iPod unit. Of this amount, only about $4, or 2.8% of the total cost, was attributable to the Chinese workers who assembled it; the rest of the costs were attributable to the numerous firms involved in making the parts (for example, Japanese firms provided the highest-value components—the hard drive and the display).[19] From a trade aspect, U.S. trade data would have recorded the full value of each iPod unit imported from China at $144 (excluding shipping costs) as originating from China, even though the value added in China was quite small. The retail price of the iPod sold in the United States was $299, meaning that there was a mark-up of about $155 per unit, which was attributable to transportation costs, retail and distributor margins, and Apple's profits. The study estimated that Apple earned at least $80 on each unit it sold in its stores, making it the single largest beneficiary (in terms of gross profit) of the sale of the iPod. The study concluded that Apple's innovation in developing and engineering the iPod and its ability to source most of its production to low-cost countries, such as China, has helped enable it to become a highly competitive and profitable firm (as well as a source for high-paying jobs in the United States). The iPod example illustrates that the rapidly changing nature of global supply chains has made it increasing difficult to interpret the implications of U.S. trade data. Such data may show where products are being imported from, but they often fail to reflect who benefits from that trade. Thus, in many instances, U.S. imports from China are really imports from many countries.

U.S.-CHINA INVESTMENT TIES[20]

Investment plays a large and growing role in U.S.-China commercial ties.[21] China's investment in U.S. assets can be broken down into several categories, including holdings of U.S. securities, foreign direct investment (FDI), and other non-bond investments. A significant share of China's investment in the United States is comprised of U.S. securities, while FDI constitutes the bulk of U.S. investment in China. The Treasury Department defines foreign holdings of U.S. securities as "U.S. securities owned by foreign residents (including banks and other institutions) except where the owner has a direct investment relationship with the U.S. issuer of the securities." U.S. statutes define FDI as "the ownership or control, directly or indirectly, by one foreign resident of 10% or more of the voting securities of an incorporated U.S. business enterprise or the equivalent interest in an unincorporated U.S. business enterprise, including a branch."[22] BEA reports data on FDI flows to and from the United States.[23] China has also invested in a number of U.S. companies, projects, and various ventures which do meet the U.S. definition of FDI, and thus, are not reflected in BEA's data.

China's Holdings of U.S. Public and Private Securities[24]

China's holdings of U.S. public and private securities are significant.[25] These include U.S. Treasury securities, U.S. government agency (such as Freddie Mac and Fannie Mae) securities, corporate securities, and equities (such as stocks). China's large holdings of U.S. securities can be largely attributed to its policy of intervening in exchange rate markets to limit the appreciation of its currency to the U.S. dollar (discussed in more detail below). For example, the Chinese government requires Chinese exporters (who are often paid in dollars) to turn over their dollars in exchange for Chinese currency. As a result, the Chinese government has accumulated a significant amount of dollars.[26] Rather than holding onto U.S. dollars, which earn no interest, the Chinese government has chosen to invest many of them into U.S. Treasury securities because they are seen as a relatively safe investment.[27] China's investment in public and private U.S. securities totaled $1.6 trillion as of June 2012.[28]

U.S. Treasury securities, which help the federal government finance its budget deficit, are the largest category of U.S. securities held by China.29 As indicated in Table 5 and Figure 5, China's holdings of U.S. Treasury securities increased from $118 billion in 2002 to $1.3 trillion as of November 2013, making China the largest foreign holder of U.S. Treasury securities (it overtook Japan as the largest holder in 2008). China's holdings of U.S. Treasury securities as a share of total foreign holdings rose from 9.6% in 2002 to 26.1% in 2010 (year-end), declined to 23.0% in 2011 and to 21.7% in 2012, and then rose to 23.0% as of November 2013.

Some analysts have raised concerns that China's large holdings of U.S. debt securities could give China leverage over U.S. foreign policy, including trade policy. They argue, for example, China might attempt to sell (or threaten to sell) a large share of its U.S. debt securities as punishment over a policy dispute, which could damage the U.S. economy. Others counter that China's holdings of U.S. debt give it very little practical leverage over the United States. They argue that, given China's economic dependency on a stable and growing U.S. economy, and its substantial holdings of U.S. securities, any attempt to try to sell a large share of those holdings would likely damage both the U.S. and Chinese economies. Such a move could also cause the U.S. dollar to sharply depreciate against global currencies, which could reduce the value of China's remaining holdings of U.S. dollar assets. Analysts also note that, while China is the largest foreign owner of U.S. Treasury Securities, those holdings are equal to only 10.4% of total U.S. public debt (as of December 2012). Finally, it is argued that, as long as China continues to largely peg the RMB to the U.S. dollar, it has little choice but to purchase U.S. dollar assets in order to maintain that peg.

Table 5. China's Holdings of U.S. Treasury Securities: 2002-November 2013

	2002	2004	2006	2008	2010	2011	2012	Nov. 2013
China's Holdings ($ billions)	118.0	222.9	396.9	727.4	1,160.1	1,151.9	1,202.8	1,317
China's Holdings as a Percent of Total Foreign Holdings	9.6%	12.1%	18.9%	23.6%	26.1%	23.0%	21.7%	23.0%

Source: U.S. Treasury Department.
Note: Data for 2002-2012 are year-end.

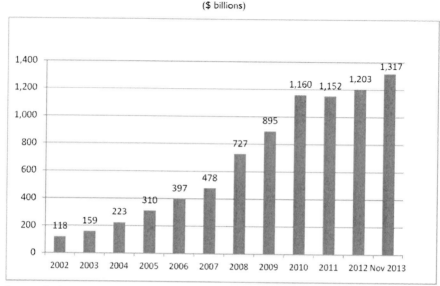

Source: U.S. Department of the Treasury.
Note: Data for 2002-2012 are year-end.

Figure 5. China's Holdings of U.S. Treasury Securities: 2002-November 2013.

In the 112th Congress, the conference report accompanying the National Defense Authorization Act of FY2012 (H.R. 1540, P.L. 112-81) included a provision requiring the Secretary of Defense to conduct a national security risk assessment of U.S. federal debt held by China. The Secretary of Defense issued a report in July 2012, stating that "attempting to use U.S. Treasury securities as a coercive tool would have limited effect and likely would do more harm to China than to the United States."As the threat is not credible and the effect would be limited even if carried out, it does not offer China deterrence options, whether in the diplomatic, military, or economic realms, and this would remain true both in peacetime and in scenarios of crisis or war.[30]

Bilateral Foreign Direct Investment Flows

The level of foreign direct investment (FDI) flows between China and the United States is relatively small given the large volume of trade between the two countries.[31] Many analysts contend that an expansion of bilateral FDI could greatly expand commercial ties.

The U.S. Bureau of Economic Analysis (BEA) is the main federal agency that collects data on FDI flows to and from the United States.[32] Its data indicate that U.S. FDI in China is significantly higher than China's FDI in the United States.[33] BEA reports that the stock of U.S. FDI in China through 2012 was $51.4 billion, down from $59.0 billion in 2010, reflecting an outflow of funds (divestment) from China back to the United States.[34] BEA estimates that U.S. majority-owned affiliates in China employed 1.4 million workers in China in 2011, of which 690,000 were in manufacturing.[35]

BEA's main FDI data measurement puts the stock of Chinese FDI in the United States through the end of 2012 at $5.2 billion on a historical-cost (or book value) basis. In 2012, Chinese FDI flows to the United States were $1.4 billion. However, these data do not reflect FDI that Chinese investors may have made through offshore locations (such as Hong Kong) to invest in the United States. To reflect this, the BEA attempts to measure the level of FDI inflows according to the country of "ultimate beneficial owner" (UBO). These measurements nearly double the estimated level of Chinese FDI in the United States. On a UBO basis, cumulative Chinese FDI in the United States through 2012 was $10.5 billion (see Table 6). As indicated in Figure 6, the stock of Chinese FDI in the United States on a UBO basis has risen sharply since 2009.

Table 6. U.S. Data on Annual U.S.–China Bilateral FDI Flows: 2005-2012 and Cumulative Value of FDI at Year-End 2012 ($ millions)

	2005	2006	2007	2008	2009	2010	2011	2012	Cumulative: Value of FDI at 2012 Year-End
China's FDI in the United States	146	315	8	500	500	1,037	520	1,370	5,154 ($10,465)*
U.S. FDI in China	1,955	4,226	5,243	15,971	- 7,512	5,240	- 1,087	- 3,482	51,363

Source: U.S. Bureau of Economic Analysis.
Notes: Cumulative data are on a historical-cost basis.
* Data in parenthesis are BEA estimates of Chinese FDI in the United States that is made by Chinese investors both directly or through other countries, described as the "country of ultimate beneficial owner" (UBO).

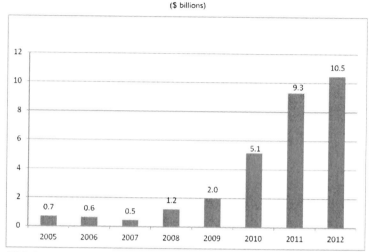

Source: U.S. Bureau of Economic Analysis.
Notes: Data is on a historic-cost basis. UBO data represents estimates of the country of origin of the entity that ultimately owns or controls the U.S. affiliate.

Figure 6. BEA's Estimate of Cumulative Chinese FDI in the United States on a UBO Basis: 2005-2012.

Some analysts contend that the BEA's data on China's FDI in the United States do not fully capture all investments. For example, the Rhodium Group (a private research consultancy and advisory company) estimates that annual Chinese FDI in the United States rose from $1.9 billion in 2009 to $7.1 billion in 2012, to $14 billion in 2013. They estimate the stock of Chinese FDI in the United States from 2000 to 2012 at $23.6 billion (and through 2013 at $35.9 billion).[36] As indicated in **Figure 7**, Rhodium Group's estimates of the stock of Chinese FDI in the United States are significantly higher than BEA's data.

CHINESE COMPANIES IN THE UNITED STATES

Although the level of Chinese FDI in the United States is relatively small, many Chinese firms view the United States as a key part of their efforts to become more globally competitive companies, move closer to their U.S. customers, circumvent perceived trade and investment barriers (such as the Buy American Act), and avoid U.S. trade remedy measures (such as antidumping duties). Some examples of Chinese FDI in the United States include the following:

The Dalian Wanda Group Corporation Ltd. on May 21, 2011, announced that it had signed a merger and acquisition agreement to acquire AMC Entertainment (the world's second-largest theater chain) for $2.6 billion.

Suntech Power Holdings Co., Ltd., the world's largest producer of solar panels, opened a solar plant in Goodyear, Arizona, in October 2010, employing 100 workers. However, in March 2013, the company announced it planned to close the plant, citing higher production costs exacerbated by U.S. anti-dumping import duties imposed on solar cells and aluminum, as well as global solar module oversupply.[37]

Sany Group, a global producer of construction equipment, founded Sany America Inc. in 2006, headquartered in Peachtree City, Georgia. In 2007, it announced it would invest $100 million to create and establish a manufacturing facility for constructing and engineering Sany products, with expected employment of 300 workers by the time the project is completed.[38]

Wanxiang Group, an automotive parts manufacturer, established Wanxiang America Corporation in 1994, based in Illinois. Over the past decade, Wanxiang America reportedly has purchased or invested in more than 20 U.S. firms and employs 5,000 U.S. workers—more than any other Chinese company.[39] In January 2013, Wanxiang America acquired nearly all of A123 Systems, a manufacturer of advanced lithium-ion batteries, for $256.6 million.

Pacific Centuries Motor (now a subsidiary of AVIC Automobile Industry Co., Ltd, a state-owned firm) purchased Nexteer Automotive, a Michigan-based firm that producers steering and driveline systems, for an estimated $450 million.[40]

Tianjin Pipe Corporation, China's largest steel pipe-maker, announced in 2009 that it planned to spend $1 billion to construct a mini-mill facility in Gregory, Texas, that will manufacture steel products from recycled scrap steel. Over the first 10 years of operation, the project is projected to boost the local economy by $2.7 billion and generate $327 million in direct employee salaries.[41]

Haier Group, a major global appliance and electronics firm, maintains its corporate headquarters for Haier America in New York City, has sales offices in 13 U.S. states, and operates a $40 million refrigerator plant in Camden, South Carolina (employing 120 people), reportedly the first U.S. manufacturing facility built by a Chinese firm (2000).

ZTE Corporation, one of China's largest telecommunications manufacturers, established a U.S. presence in 1995. ZTE USA is headquartered in Dallas, Texas, and maintains R&D facilities in five U.S. states.

Huawei Technologies is a leading global information and communications technology solutions provider. Since gaining a U.S. presence in 2011, Huawei has reportedly partnered with 280 U.S. technology providers, with total procurement contracts exceeding $30 billion, covering such items as software, components, chipsets, and services. In February 2012, Huawei announced procurement contracts with U.S. firms worth $6 billion.[42]

Golden Dragon Precise Copper Tube Group Inc., one of the world's largest precise copper tube manufacturers, announced in February 2012 that it planned to build a $100 million manufacturing facility in Alabama.

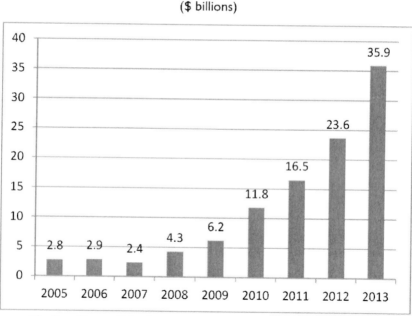

Source: Rhodium Group, China Investment Monitor.
Notes: Data are on a UBO basis and are derived from a number of sources, including commercial databases, media reports, and industry contacts in China.

Figure 7. Rhodium Group's Estimates of Cumulative Chinese FDI in the United States on a UBO Basis: 2005-2013.

In addition to China's FDI in the United States and its holdings in U.S. Treasury securities, China (as of June 2012) held $221 billion in U.S. equities (such as stocks), up from $3 billion in June 2005. It also held $202 billion in U.S. agency securities, many of which are asset-backed (such as Fannie Mae and Freddie Mac securities),[43] and $22 billion in corporate bonds. The China Investment Corporation (CIC), a sovereign wealth fund established by the Chinese government in 2007 with $200 billion in registered capital to help better manage China's foreign exchange reserves, had financial assets totaling $482 billion at the end of 2011. CIC has been one of the largest Chinese purchasers of U.S. equities and other U.S. assets; it has stakes in such firms as Morgan Stanley, the Blackstone Group, and J.C. Flowers & Co.[44] It appears that many of the investments by the CIC and other Chinese entities have attempted to avoid political controversy in the United States by limiting their ownership shares to less than 10%.

Issues Raised by Chinese FDI in the United States

Many U.S. analysts contend that greater Chinese FDI in the United States, especially in "greenfield" projects (new ventures) that manufacture products or provide services in the United States and create new jobs for U.S. workers,[45] could help improve bilateral economic relations and might lessen perceptions among some critics in the United States that growing U.S.-China trade undermines U.S. employment and harms U.S. economic interests.[46] A number of analysts note that China's outward FDI has been growing rapidly since 2004 and is likely to continue in the years ahead.[47]

Such analysts contend that greater efforts should be made by U.S. policy makers to encourage Chinese firms to invest in the United States rather than block them for political reasons. In June 2011, President Obama issued an executive order establishing the "SelectUSA Initiative" to coordinate federal efforts to promote and retain investment in the United States. According to a White House factsheet issued during the U.S. visit of Chinese Vice President Xi Jinping in February 2012, China was already one of SelectUSA top 10 focus markets, and the Administration was planning a significant expansion of the initiative, including with resources dedicated to attracting Chinese investors and facilitating their investment. The two sides further pledged to deepen cooperation on infrastructure financing.[48] At the July 2013 session of the U.S.-China S&ED, the United States pledged to welcome investment from China, including those made by Chinese state-owned enterprises (SOEs).

Some critics of China's current FDI policies and practices contend that they are largely focused on mergers and acquisitions that are geared toward boosting the competitive position of Chinese firms and enterprises favored by the Chinese government for development (some of which also may be receiving government subsidies). Some argue that such investments are often made largely to obtain technology and know-how for Chinese firms, but do little to boost the U.S. economy by, for example, building new factories and hiring workers. Another major issue relating to Chinese FDI in the United States is the relative lack of transparency of Chinese firms, especially in terms of their connections to the central government. When Chinese SOEs attempt to purchase U.S. company assets, some U.S. analysts ask what role government officials in Beijing played in that decision. Chinese officials contend that investment decisions by Chinese companies, including SOEs and publicly held firms (where the government is the largest shareholder), are solely based on commercial considerations, and have criticized U.S. investment policies as "protectionist."

According to the Foreign Investment and National SecurityAct (FINSA) of 2007 (P.L. 110-149), the Committee on Foreign Investment in the United States (CFIUS) may conduct an investigation on the effect of an investment transaction on national security if the covered transaction is a foreign government-controlled transaction (in addition to if the transaction threatens to impair national security, or results in the control of a critical piece of U.S. infrastructure by a foreign person).[49] The House report on the bill (H.Rept. 110-24, H.R. 556) noted: "The Committee believes that acquisitions by certain government-owned companies do create heightened national security concerns, particularly where government-owned companies make decisions for inherently governmental—as opposed to commercial—reasons."

There have been several instances in which efforts by Chinese firms (oftentimes these have been SOEs or state-favored firms) have raised concerns of some U.S. policy makers and/or U.S. stakeholders:

- On January 23, 2014, Lenovo, a Chinese technology company, announced that it would purchase IBM's x86 server business for $2.3 billion. On January 29, 2014, Lenovo announced that it would acquire Motorola Mobility from Google for $2.9 billion.
- On May 29, 2013, Shuanghui International Holdings, the majority owner of China's largest meat processing enterprise (Henan Shuanghui Investment & Development Company), announced it was seeking to purchase Smithfield Foods, the largest U.S. pork producer,

for $7.1 billion (including the assumption of Smithfield's debt). If the merger goes through, it would represent the largest acquisition of a U.S. firm by a Chinese company to date. The proposed acquisition has raised a number of concerns among some U.S. policy makers.[50] On June 20, 2013, 15 members of the Senate Committee on Agricultural, Nutrition, and Forestry sent a letter to the U.S. Secretary of the Treasury contending that the U.S. food supply is "critical infrastructure" and should be regarded as a national security issue during the CFIUS review process, urging that the Department of Agriculture and the Food and Drug Administration be represented in any CFIUS review of the transaction, and stating that review look to broader issues, including food security, food safety, and biosecurity.[51] The Senate Agriculture Committee also announced plans to hold a hearing on the transaction and to "more broadly examine how the government review process of foreign acquisitions of U.S. companies addresses American food safety, protection of American technologies, and intellectual property, and the effects of increased foreign ownership of the U.S. food supply."[52] In a June 21, 2013, letter to Administration officials, Senators Max Baucus and Orrin Hatch stated that the planned acquisition "has thrown a spotlight on China's unjustified trade barriers to U.S. meat exports."[53] A letter sent to Administration officials by Representative Rosa DeLauro and Senator Elizabeth Warren about the planned acquisition on June 26, 2013, raised a number of issues relating to food security, food safety, intellectual property rights protection, unfair Chinese trade practices, and U.S. global economic competitiveness and requested the Obama Administration to publicly respond to eight major concerns.[54] On July 10, 2013, the Senate Committee on Agricultural, Nutrition, and Forestry held a hearing on the proposed transaction. On September 26, 2013, Shuanghui International Holdings completed its purchase of Smithfield.

- In January 2013, Wanxiang America Corporation completed its acquisition of substantially all nongovernment business assets of A123 Systems, a manufacturer of lithium battery products. The acquisition included A123's automotive, grid, and commercial business assets, including technology, products, customer contracts, and U.S. facilities in Michigan, Massachusetts, and Missouri; its manufacturing operations in China; and its equity interest in Shanghai Advanced Traction Battery Systems Company (A123's joint venture with Shanghai Automotive).⁵⁵ Several Members of Congress expressed concerns over the national security implications of Wanxiang's acquisition of A123 Systems, as well as concerns that U.S. government grants that had been given to A123 Systems in the past might end up benefiting a Chinese company.

- On October 8, 2012, the chairman and ranking Member of the House Intelligence Committee (Representatives Mike Rogers and C.A. Dutch Ruppersberger) released a report recommending that U.S. companies considering doing business with Chinese telecommunications companies Huawei and ZTE to find another vendor, and that the CFIUS should block acquisitions, takeovers, or mergers involving Huawei and ZTE given "the threat to U.S. national security interests." The report went on to state that "we have serious concerns about Huawei and ZTE, and their connection to the communist government of China. China is known to be the major perpetrator of cyber espionage, and Huawei and ZTE failed to alleviate serious concerns throughout this important investigation."⁵⁶
- On September 28, 2012, President Obama issued an executive order requiring Ralls Corporation, a Chinese-owned firm, to divest its interest in four wind farm project companies in Oregon that it acquired earlier in the year, due to national security concerns, reportedly because of their proximity to a naval test facility.⁵⁷ China's government-controlled media called the action "protectionist."
- On May 9, 2012, the Federal Reserve announced that it had approved (1) the application by Industrial and Commercial Bank of China Limited, China Investment Corporation, and Central Huijin Investment Ltd., to become bank holding companies by acquiring up to 80% of the voting shares of the Bank of East Asia (USA) National Association; (2) the Bank of China's application to establish a branch in Chicago, IL; and (3) the application by the Agricultural Bank of China Limited to establish a state-licensed branch in New York City.⁵⁸ In a letter to Federal Reserve Chairman Ben Bernanke, Senator Robert Casey noted that each of the entities approved by the Federal Reserve was state-owned, and he expressed concern that "these banks and their U.S. subsidiaries will use their state-support as a way to underprice U.S. banks that abide by U.S. law and do not have the support of a sovereign country behind them."⁵⁹
- In May 2010, Huawei bought certain intellectual property assets of 3Leaf Systems (an insolvent U.S. technology firm) for $2 million. A

February 2011 letter issued by Senators Jim Webb and Jon Kyl to then-Commerce Secretary Gary Locke and then-Treasury Secretary Tim Geithner stated: "We are convinced that any attempt Huawei makes to expand its presence in the U.S. or acquire U.S. companies warrants thorough scrutiny. Moreover, the 3Leaf acquisition appears certain to generate transfer to China by Huawei of advanced U.S. computing technology. Allowing Huawei and, by extension, communist China to have access to this core technology could pose a serious risk as U.S. computer networks come to further rely on and integrate this technology."[60] In February 2011, Huawei stated that it been formally notified by CFIUS that it should withdraw its application to acquire 3Leaf's assets, which it later did.[61] In an "Open Letter," Huawei invited the U.S. government to carry out a formal investigation on any concerns it may have about Huawei.[62]

- In May 2010, Anshan Iron and Steel Group Corporation (Ansteel), a major Chinese state-owned steel producer, announced plans to form a joint venture with Steel Development Company, a U.S. firm in Mississippi, to build and operate four mills to produce reinforcing bar and other bar products used in infrastructure applications, and one mill that would be capable of producing electrical and silicon grades of steel used in energy applications.[63] In July 2010, the Congressional Steel Caucus sent a letter signed by 50 Members to Secretary of the Treasury Tim Geithner, expressing concerns over the effect the investment would have "on American jobs and our national security."[64] At a February 2012 hearing on China's SOEs, Representative Visclosky, chairman of the Congressional Steel Caucus stated: "As a Caucus, we were concerned that the investment would allow a Chinese state-owned enterprise to pursue the government of China's aims, and not the aims of the employer, the American worker, or the market. We were concerned that this investment would allow the full force and financing of the Chinese government to exploit the American steel market fromAmerican soil. We also were concerned that China would have access to new steel production technologies and information regardingAmerican national security infrastructure projects."[65]

- In February 2010, Emcore Corporation, a provider of compound semiconductor-based components, subsystems, and systems for the fiber optics and solar power markets, announced it had agreed to sell 60% interest in its fiber optics business (excluding its satellite

communications and specialty photonics fiber optics businesses) to China's Tangshan Caofeidian Investment Corporation (TCIC) for $27.8 million. However, Emcore announced in June 2010 that the deal had been ended because of concerns by CFIUS.[66]
- In July 2009, China's Northwest Nonferrous International Investment Company, a Chinese SOE, made a $26 million offer to purchase a 51% stake in the Firstgold Corporation, a U.S. exploration-stage company. However, the deal reportedly raised national concerns within CFUIS because some of the mines controlled by Firstgold were near U.S. military installations. As a result, the Chinese firm withdrew its bid in December 2009.[67]
- In September 2007, Huawei announced plans, along with its partner, Bain Capital Partners, to buy the U.S. firm 3Com Corporation, a provider of data networking equipment, for $2.2 billion. However, the proposed merger was withdrawn in February 2008 following a review of the deal by CFIUS when Huawei and its partner failed to adequately address U.S. national security concerns raised by CFIUS members.[68]

In 2005, the China National Offshore Oil Corporation (CNOOC), a Chinese SOE, made a bid to buy UNOCAL, a U.S. energy company, for $18.5 billion, but widespread opposition in Congress led CNOOC to withdraw its bid. Some Members argued at the time that the proposed takeover represented a clear threat to the energy and national security of the United States, would put vital oil assets in the Gulf of Mexico and Alaska into the hands of a Chinese state-controlled company, could transfer a host of highly advanced technologies to China, and that CNOOC's bid to take over UNOCAL would be heavily subsidized by the Chinese government. Some Members argued that "vital" U.S. energy assets should never sold to the Chinese government. CNOOC officials referred to U.S. political opposition to the sale as "regrettable and unjustified."[69]
- In 2004, Lenovo Group Limited, a computer company primarily owned by the Chinese government, signed an agreement with IBM Corporation to purchase IBM's personal computer division for $1.75 billion. Some U.S. officials raised national security concerns over potential espionage activities that could occur in the United States at IBM research facilities by Lenovo employees if the deal went through. A review of the agreement by CFIUS took place in which IBM and Lenovo were able to address certain national security

concerns and, as a result, the acquisition was completed in April 2005.[70]

Chinese Restrictions on U.S. FDI in China

U.S. trade officials have urged China to liberalize its FDI regime in order to boost U.S. business opportunities in, and expand U.S. exports to, China. Although China is one of the world's top recipients of FDI, the Chinese central government imposes numerous restrictions on the level and of types of FDI allowed in China. According to the U.S.-China Business Council, China imposes ownership barriers on nearly 100 industries.[71] The OECD's 2012 FDI Regulatory Restrictiveness Index, which measures statutory restrictions on foreign direct investment in 57 countries (including all OECD and G20 countries, and covering 22 sectors), ranked China's FDI regime as the most restrictive, based on foreign equity limitations, screening or approval mechanisms, restrictions on the employment of foreigners as key personnel, and operational restrictions (such as restrictions on branching, capital repatriation, and land ownership).[72]

To a great extent, China's investment policies appear to be linked to industrial policies that seek to promote the development of sectors identified by the government as critical to future economic development. For example, since the early 1980s, the Chinese government has encouraged foreign auto companies to invest in China, but has limited FDI in that sector to 50-50 joint ventures with domestic Chinese partners.[73] In addition, the central government maintains a "Guideline Catalogue for Foreign Investment" (the latest revision was issued in January 2012), which lists FDI categories that are encouraged, restricted, or prohibited.[74] Many of the sectors under the "encouraged" category include high technology, green technology, and energy conservation, and pollution control.[75] Several of the sectors under the "restricted" category limit FDI to joint ventures (such as for rare earth smelting) or where the Chinese parties are the controlling shareholders (such as railway passenger transport companies). "Prohibited" sectors are those that fall under "national security" concerns (such as manufacturing of ammunition and weapons) or are categories where the government seeks to preserve state monopolies (such as postal companies) or protect Chinese firms from foreign competition (such as mining of rare earth elements).

The Chinese government also sets restrictions on FDI inflows during the investment screening process, or through its mergers and acquisition regulations, especially when seeking to protect pillar or strategic industries that the central government (as well as many provincial and local governments) seeks to promote. Many critics of China's investment policies contend that the Chinese government often requires foreign firms to transfer technology to their China partners, and sometimes to set up research and development facilities in China, in exchange for access to China's markets.[76] Foreign-invested firms in China face a number of challenges, including local protectionism, lack of regulatory transparency, IPR theft, and discriminatory license practices. A 2013 business survey by the American Chamber of Commerce in China (AmCham China) found that 35% of respondents stated that they were at a competitive disadvantage as a result of Chinese industrial policies that favored state-owned enterprises.[77] Some U.S. policy makers have suggested that Chinese investment in certain U.S. sectors should be restricted in response to Chinese policies that limit U.S. FDI in China in similar sectors.[78]

The United States and China have held negotiations on reaching a bilateral investment treaty (BIT) with the goal of expanding bilateral investment opportunities. U.S. negotiators hope such a treaty would improve the investment climate for U.S. firms in China by enhancing legal protections and dispute resolution procedures, and by obtaining a commitment from the Chinese government that it would treat U.S. investors no less favorably than Chinese investors. However, some groups have argued that a BIT with China could hurt U.S. workers by encouraging more U.S. firms to relocate to China.[79]

In April 2012, the Obama Administration released a "Model Bilateral Investment Treaty" that was developed to enhance U.S. objectives in the negotiation of new BITs.[80] The new BIT model establishes mechanisms to promote greater transparency, labor and environment requirements, disciplines to prevent parties from imposing domestic technology requirements, and measures to boost the ability of investors to participate in the development of standards and technical regulations on a nondiscriminatory basis.

During the July 10-11, 2013, session of the U.S.-China Strategic and Economic Dialogue (S&ED), China indicated its intention to negotiate a high-standard BIT with the United States that would include all stages of investment and all sectors, a move that U.S. officials described as "a significant breakthrough, and the first time China has agreed to do so with another country."[81] A press release by the Chinese Ministry of Commerce stated that China was willing to negotiate a BIT on the basis of non-discrimination and a negative list, meaning the agreement would identify only those sectors not open to foreign investment on a non-discriminatory basis (as opposed to a BIT with a positive list which would only list sectors open to foreign investment).

At the Communist Party of China's 3rd Plenum meeting in November 2013, the government stated that it would reduce regulations on FDI in China and create a number of free trade zones that may open up certain sectors to foreign investment.

MAJOR U.S.-CHINA TRADE ISSUES

China's economic reforms and rapid economic growth, along with the effects of globalization, have caused the economies of the United States and China to become increasingly integrated.[82] Although growing U.S.-China economic ties are considered by most analysts to be mutually beneficial overall, tensions have risen over a number of Chinese economic and trade policies that many U.S. critics charge are protectionist, economically distortive, and damaging to U.S. economic interests. According to the USTR, most U.S. trade disputes with China stem from the consequences of its incomplete transition to a free market economy. Major areas of concern for U.S. stakeholders include China's:

- Extensive network of industrial policies that seek to promote and protect domestic sectors and firms, especially SOEs, deemed by the government to be critical to the country's future economic growth;
- Failure to provide adequate protection of U.S. intellectual property rights (IPR) and (alleged) government-directed cyber security attacks against U.S. firms;
- Mixed record on implementing its obligations in the World Trade Organization (WTO) and its failure to date to join the WTO's Government Procurement Agreement (GPA); and
- Intervention in currency markets to limit the appreciation of the renminbi (RMB) against the dollar (and other major currencies) in order to make China's exports more globally competitive.

Chinese "State Capitalism"

Currently, a significant share of China's economy is thought to be driven by market forces. According to a 2010 WTO report, the private sector now accounts for more than 60% of China's gross domestic product (GDP).[83] However, the Chinese government continues to play a major role in economic decision-making. For example, at the macroeconomic level, the Chinese government maintains policies that induce households to save a high level of their income, much of which is deposited in state-controlled Chinese banks. This enables the government to provide low-cost financing to Chinese firms, especially SOEs. At the microeconomic level, the Chinese government (at the central and local government level) seeks to promote the development of industries that are deemed critical to the country's future economic development by using various policies, such as subsidies, tax breaks, preferential loans, trade barriers, FDI restrictions, discriminatory regulations and standards, export restrictions on raw materials (such as rare earths), technology transfer requirements imposed on foreign firms, public procurement rules that give preferences to domestic firms, and weak enforcement of IPR laws.

Many analysts contend that the Chinese government's intervention in various sectors through industrial policies has intensified in recent years. The December 2013 U.S. Trade Representative's (USTR's) report on China's WTO trade compliance states:

> During most of the past decade, the Chinese government emphasized the state's role in the economy, diverging from the path of economic reform that had driven China's accession to the WTO. With the state leading China's economic development, the Chinese government pursued new and more expansive industrial policies, often designed to limit market access for imported goods, foreign manufacturers and foreign service suppliers, while offering substantial government guidance, resources and regulatory support to Chinese industries, particularly ones dominated by state-owned enterprises. This heavy state role in the economy, reinforced byunchecked discretionary actions of Chinese government regulators, generated serious trade frictions with China's many trade partners, including the United States.[84]

The extent of SOE involvement in the Chinese economy is difficult to measure due to the opaque nature of the corporate sector in China and the relative lack of transparency regarding the relationship between state actors (including those at the central and non-central government levels) and Chinese firms. According to one study by the U.S.-China Economic and Security Review Commission:

> The state sector in China consists of three main components. First, there are enterprises fully owned by the state through the State-owned Assets and Supervision and Administration Commission (SASAC) of the State Council and by SASACs of provincial, municipal, and county governments. Second, there are SOEs that are majority owners of enterprises that are not officially considered SOEs but are effectively controlled by their SOE owners. Finally, there is a group of entities, owned and controlled indirectly through SOE subsidiaries based inside and outside of China. The actual size of this third group is unknown. Urban collective enterprises and government-owned township and village enterprises (TVEs) also belong to the state sector but are not considered SOEs. The state-owned and controlled portion of the Chinese economy is large. Based on reasonable assumptions, it appears that the visible state sector—SOEs and entities directly controlled by SOEs, accounted for more than 40 percent of China's nonagricultural GDP. If the contributions of indirectly controlled entities, urban collectives, and public TVEs are considered, the share of GDP owned and controlled by the state is approximately 50 percent.[85]

According to the Chinese government, at the end of 2011, there were 144,700 state-owned or state-controlled enterprises, excluding financial institutions, with total assets worth $13.6 trillion.[86] Chinese SOEs have undergone significant restructuring over the years. More than 90% of SOEs have reportedly become corporations or shareholding companies.[87] The Chinese government has identified a number of industries where the state should have full control or where the state should dominate. These include autos, aviation, banking, coal, construction, environmental technology, information technology, insurance, media, metals (such as steel), oil and gas, power, railways, shipping, telecommunications, and tobacco.[88]

Many SOEs are owned or controlled by local governments. According to one analyst:

> The typical large industrial Chinese company is...wholly or majority-owned by a local government which appoints senior management and provides free or low-cost land and utilities, tax breaks, and where possible, guarantees that locally made products will be favored by local governments, consumers, and other businesses. In return, the enterprise

provides the local state with a source of jobs for local workers, tax revenues, and dividends.[89]

China's banking system is largely controlled by state-owned or state-controlled banks. In 2011, the top five largest banks in China, all of which were shareholding companies with significant state ownership, accounted for 57.5% of Chinese banking assets. The Chinese government also has four banks that are 100% state-owned and holds shares in a number of joint stock commercial banks.[90] SOEs are believed to receive preferential credit treatment by government banks, while private firms must often pay higher interest rates or obtain credit elsewhere. According to one estimate, SOEs accounted for 85% ($1.4 trillion) of all bank loans in 2009.[91]

Not only are SOEs dominant players in China's economy, many are becoming quite large by global standards. In 2013, 84 Chinese companies (excluding Hong Kong firms) made *Fortune Magazine's Global 500* list of the world's largest firms based on revenues. Of the 84 Chinese companies listed, 77 firms or 88.1% were state-owned or state-controlled enterprises (defined as where the state owned 50% of the company). Of the 10 non-SOEs companies listed, at least 3 are partially owned by the government. For example, the government owes 26.5% of the Bank of Communications, 15.7% of China Minsheng Banking Corp., and 20% of Shanghai Pudong Development Bank.[92] Another company, Huawei (a major telecommunications company) describes itself as an employee-owned firm. However, many U.S. analysts contend that Huawei has strong links with the Chinese government, including the Chinese People's Liberation Army (PLA), and has not published a full breakdown of its ownership structure. In addition, in the past, the Chinese government reportedly ordered state banks to extend loans to the company early in its development so that it could compete against foreign firms in the domestic telecommunications market.[93]

China's Plan to Modernize the Economy and Promote Indigenous Innovation

Many of the industrial policies that China has implemented or formulated since 2006 appear to stem largely from a comprehensive document issued by China's State Council (the highest executive organ of state power) in 2006 titled the *National Medium-and Long-Term Program for Science and Technology Development (2006-2020)*, often referred to as the MLP. The MLP appears to represent an ambitious plan to modernize the structure of China's economy by transforming it from a global center of low-tech manufacturing to a major center of innovation (by the year 2020) and a global innovation leader by 2050.[94] It also seeks to sharply reduce the country's dependence on foreign technology. The MLP includes the stated goals of "indigenous innovation, leapfrogging in priority fields, enabling development, and leading the future."[95] Some of the broad goals of the MLP state that by 2020:

- The progress of science and technology will contribute 60% or above to China's development.
- The country's reliance on foreign technology will decline to 30% or below (from an estimated current level of 50%).
- Gross expenditures for research and development (R&D) would rise to 2.5% of gross domestic product (from 1.3% in 2005). Priority areas for increased R&D include space programs, aerospace development and manufacturing, renewable energy, computer science, and life sciences.[96]

The document states that "China must place the strengthening of indigenous innovative capability at the core of economic restructuring, growth model change, and national competitiveness enhancement. Building an innovation-oriented country is therefore a major strategic choice for China's future development." This goal, according to the document, is to be achieved by formulating and implementing regulations in the country's government procurement law to "encourage and protect indigenous innovation," establishing a coordination mechanism for government procurement of indigenous innovative products, requiring a first-buy policy for major domestically made high-tech equipment and products that possess proprietary intellectual property rights, providing policy support to enterprises in procuring domestic high-tech equipment, and developing "relevant technology standards" through government procurement.

Reaction by U.S. Stakeholders

Beginning in 2009, several U.S. companies began to raise concerns over a number of Chinese government circulars that would establish an "Indigenous Innovation Product Accreditation" system. For example, in November 2009, the Chinese government released a "Circular on Launching the 2009 National Indigenous Innovation Product Accreditation Work," requiring companies to file applications by December 2009 for their products to be considered for accreditation as "indigenous innovation products." Similar proposed circulars were issued at the provincial and local government levels as well. U.S.

business representatives expressed deep concern over the circulars, arguing that they were protectionist in nature because they extended preferential treatment for Chinese government procurement to domestic Chinese firms that developed and owned intellectual property (IP) and thus largely excluded foreign firms.[97] AmCham China described China's attempt to link IP ownership with market access as "unprecedented worldwide."[98] A letter written by the U.S. Chamber of Commerce and 33 business associations to the Chinese government on December 10, 2009, stated that the indigenous innovations circulars would "make it virtually impossible for any non-Chinese companies to participate in China's government procurement market—even those that have made substantial and long-term investments in China, employ Chinese citizens, and pay taxes to the Chinese government."[99] Such groups contend that a large share of their technology is developed globally and thus it would be difficult to attribute the share of technology developed in China needed to obtain accreditation.[100]

A 2011 AmCham China survey found that 40% of respondents believed that China's indigenous innovation policies would hurt their businesses and 26% said their businesses were already being hurt by such policies. At a November 2011 WTO review of China's IPR policies, the U.S. WTO representative stated that China's policies of adopting indigenous innovation had "created a troubling trend toward increased discriminatory policies which were aimed at coercing technology transfer." He stated that "Chinese regulations, rules and other regulatory measures frequently called for technology transfer, and in certain cases, conditioned, or proposed to condition, the eligibility for government benefits or preferences on intellectual property being owned or developed in China, or being licensed, in some cases exclusively, to a Chinese party."[101]

China's Response to U.S. Concerns

The Chinese government responded to U.S. concerns over its indigenous innovation policies by arguing that they did not discriminate against foreign firms or violate global trade rules.[102] However, during the visit of (then) Chinese President Hu Jintao to the United States in January 2011, the Chinese government stated that it would not link its innovation policies to the provision of government procurement preferences.[103] During the May 2011 session of the U.S.-China Strategic and Economic Dialogue (S&ED), China pledged that it would eliminate all of its indigenous innovation products catalogs.[104] During the November 2011 talks held under the U.S.-China Joint Commission on Commerce and Trade (JCCT), the Chinese government announced that the

State Council had issued a measure requiring governments of provinces, municipalities, and autonomous regions to eliminate by December 1, 2011, any catalogues or other measures linking innovation policies to government procurement preferences.[105] This occurred after foreign business groups raised concerns that discriminatory indigenous innovation policies might continue to be implemented at the local level even after Hu Jintao's commitment. For example, The U.S.-China Business Council (USCBC) reported in February 2011 that it had identified 22 municipal and provincial governments that had issued at least 61 indigenous innovation catalogues. U.S. business representatives sought to ensure that Beijing's pledge on indigenous innovation would apply at all levels of government in China.

In May 2013, the USCBC reported that, although the central government had largely been successful in ensuring that sub-national governments complied with implement Hu Jintao's January 2011 commitments, 13 provinces had not yet issued any measures to comply.[106] In addition, an October 2012 USCBC survey found that 85% of respondents said they had seen little impact on their businesses resulting from China's commitments delinking indigenous innovation with government procurement.[107]

Remaining U.S. Concerns

While many U.S. business leaders have applauded China's pledge to delink indigenous innovation from government procurement, some remain wary that China will implement new policies that attempt to provide preferences to local Chinese firms over foreign firms. According to Adam Segal with the Council on Foreign Relations: "Even if China reverses certain policies under U.S. pressure, it will remain dedicated to those goals. U.S. policy is likely to become a game of Whac-a-Mole, beating down one Chinese initiative on indigenous innovation only to see another pop up."[108] U.S. business groups are also concerned with how the MLP blueprint will affect China's commitment to enforcing foreign IPR. They note, for example, that the MLP states: "Indigenous innovation refers to enhancing original innovation, integrated innovation, and re-innovation based on assimilation and absorption of imported technology, in order to improve our national innovation capability." To some, this seems to indicate that China intends to take existing technology, make some changes and improvements on it, and then claim it as its own without acknowledging or compensating the original IPR holders. A 2011 report by the U.S. Chamber of Commerce stated that China's indigenous innovation policies led many international technology companies to conclude that the MLP is a "blueprint for technology theft on a scale the world has never seen before."[109]

U.S. officials have attempted to convince Beijing that, while its desire to increase innovation in China is a commendable goal, its efforts to limit the participation of foreign firms in such efforts, or attempting to condition market access in China to the development of IPR by foreign firms in China will hinder, not promote, the advancement of innovation in China. The direction China takes on this issue could have a significant impact on U.S. economic interests as noted by a study by the U.S. International Trade Commission (USITC):

> To the extent that China's policies succeed in accelerating technological progress, productivity, and innovation in the Chinese economy, they could provide spillover benefits for other countries. But if indigenous innovation policies act as a form of technological import substitution, systematically favoring Chinese domestic firms over foreign firms in relevant industries, they would be expected to have a negative effect on foreign firms and economies roughly analogous to what would occur if China simply imposed a protective tariff on imports of goods in the relevant sectors or levied a discriminatory excise tax on the sales of FIEs in the Chinese market.[110]

Intellectual Property Rights (IPR)

U.S. business and government representatives have voiced growing concern over economic losses suffered by U.S. firms as a result of IPR infringement in China (and elsewhere), including those that have resulted from cyber-attacks. U.S. innovation and the intellectual property that is generated by such activities have been cited by various economists as a critical source of U.S. economic growth and global competitiveness.[111] For example, according to the Department of Commerce, in 2010, U.S. IP-intensive industries supported at least 40 million jobs and contributed $5.1 trillion (or 34.8%) to U.S. gross domestic product (GDP).[112] A study by NDP Consulting estimated that in 2008, workers in IP-intensive production earned 60% more than workers at similar levels in non-IP industries.[113] A study on the Apple iPod concluded that Apple's innovation in developing and engineering the iPod and its ability to source most of its production to low-cost countries, such as China, have helped enable it to become a highly competitive and profitable firm as well as a creator of high-paying jobs (such as engineers engaged in the design of Apple products) in the United States.[114]

Lack of effective and consistent protection of IPR has been cited by U.S. firms as one of the most significant problems they face in doing business in China. Other U.S. firms have expressed concern over pressures they often face from Chinese government entities to share technology and IPR with a Chinese partner. Although China has significantly improved its IPR protection regime over the past few years, U.S. IP industries complain that piracy rates in China continue to remain unacceptably high and economic losses are significant, as illustrated by studies and estimates made by several stakeholders:

- A May 2013 study by the Commission on the Theft of American Intellectual Property estimated the annual cost to the U.S. economy of global IPR theft at $300 billion, of which China accounted for 50% ($150 billion) to 80% ($240 billion) of those losses.[115]
- A 2013 AmCham China survey found that 72% of respondents said that China's IPR enforcement was either ineffective or totally ineffective.[116]
- The USITC estimated that U.S. intellectual property-intensive firms that conducted business in China lost $48.2 billion in sales, royalties, and license fees in 2009 because of IPR violations there. It also estimated that an effective IPR enforcement regime in China that was comparable to U.S. levels could increase employment by IP-intensive firms in the United States by 923,000 jobs.[117]
- The Business Software Alliance (BSA) estimated the commercial value of illegally used software in China at $8.9 billion in 2011 (up from $6.7 billion in 2007) and that the software piracy rate in China was 77% (down from 82% in 2007).[118] BSA further estimated that legitimate software sales in China were only $2.7 billion, compared to legal sales of $41.7 billion in the United States.
- The U.S. Customs and Border Protection reported that China accounted for 72% of pirated goods seized by the agency in FY2012 (based on domestic value). The value of seized goods originating from China and Hong Kong was $1.1 billion.[119] Handbags and wallets accounted for nearly half the estimated value of seized goods originating in China.

Chinese officials contend that they have significantly improved their IPR protection regime, but argue that the country lacks the resources and a sophisticated legal system to effectively deal with IPR violations. They also contend that IPR infringement is a serious problem for domestic Chinese firms as well. However, some analysts contend that China's relatively poor record on IPR enforcement can be partially explained by the fact that Chinese leaders want to make China a major producer of capital-intensive and high-technology products, and thus, they are tolerant of IPR piracy if it helps Chinese firms become more technologically advanced. According to an official at the U.S. Chamber of Commerce:

> The newer and emerging challenge to U.S. IPR is not a function of China's lack of political will to crackdown on infringers. Rather, it is a manifestation of a coherent, and government-directed, or at least government-motivated, strategy to lessen China's perceived reliance on foreign innovations and IP. China is actively working to create a legal environment that enables it to intervene in the market for IP, help its own companies to "re-innovate" competing IPR as a substitute to American and other foreign technologies, and potentially misappropriate U.S. and other foreign IP as components of its industrial policies and internal market regulation.... The common themes throughout these policies are: 1) undermine and displace foreign IP; 2) leverage China's large domestic market to develop national champions and promote its own IP, displacing foreign competitors in China; and 3) building on China's domestic successes by displacing competitors in foreign markets.[120]

An illustration of alleged IPR theft in China involves American Superconductor Corporation (AMSC). On September 14, 2011, AMSC announced that it was filing criminal and civil complaints in China against Sinovel Wind Group Co. Ltd. (Sinovel), China's largest wind turbine producer, and other parties, alleging the illegal use of AMSC's intellectual property. According to an AMSC press release, Sinovel illegally obtained and used AMSC's wind turbine control software code to upgrade its 1.5 megawatt wind turbines in the field to meet proposed Chinese grid codes and to potentially allow for the use of core electrical components from other manufacturers.[121] In addition, AMSC claimed that Sinovel had refused to pay for past shipments from AMSC and was now refusing to honor contracts for future shipments of components and spare parts as well.[122] AMSC has brought several civil cases against Sinovel, seeking to recover more than $1.2 billion for contracted shipments and damages caused by Sinovel's contract breaches.[123]

According to a specialist in intellectual property at Tufts University, "Chinese companies, once they acquire the needed technology, will often abandon their Western partners on the pretext the technology or product failed to meet Chinese governmental regulations. This is yet another example of a Chinese industrial policy aimed at procuring, by virtually any means, technology in order to provide Chinese domestic industries with a competitive advantage."[124]

During the December 2010 U.S.-China Joint Commission on Commerce and Trade (JCCT),[125] the Chinese government announced several new initiatives to improve its IPR protection regime, including boosting purchases of legitimate software by government agencies and 30 large SOEs. The USTR's 2011 *Special 301* report (an annual review of IPR and market access practices in foreign countries) noted that China had launched the "Program for Special Campaign on Combating IPR Infringement and Manufacture and Sales of Counterfeiting and Shoddy Commodities" (Special Campaign) in October 2010, aimed at a broad range of IPR violations. The Special Campaign involved 26 member agencies (led by a Chinese vice premier), and reportedly led to improved government coordination of IPR enforcement by the Chinese government.

The USTR's 2012 *Special 301* report stated that, while China had made some notable improvements to its IPR enforcement regime (in particular by making the Special Campaign on IPR enforcement permanent), serious problems remain. These include very high levels of trademark counterfeiting and copyright piracy, the persistence of "notorious" physical and online markets selling IPR-infringing goods, the manufacturing and sale of counterfeit pharmaceuticals, export of counterfeit goods, and discriminatory policies seeking to promote indigenous innovation in China by coercing foreign firms to transfer IPR to Chinese domestic firms. The USTR further noted a "recent alarming increase" in thefts of trade secrets (both in China and outside China) for the benefit of Chinese entities. Many of these problems, according to the USTR, stemmed from the lack of an effective government deterrent to such activities. In addition, while China's campaign to require central and provincial governments to use legitimate software produced a "modest increase" in U.S. software sales to the Chinese government, piracy rates by Chinese SOEs remained high.[126]

The USTR's 2013 Special 301 report stated that China had made comprehensive improvements to its trade laws and regulations, but indicated growing U.S. concern over the apparent growth of trade secret theft in China, including those involving departing employees, failed joint ventures, cyber intrusion and hacking (discussed in more detail below), and misuse of information submitted by U.S. firms to Chinese government entities for purposes of complying with regulatory obligations.[127] The USTR also noted that IPR enforcement remains a serious problem and has gotten worse because of cyber theft (discussed in more detail below). The USTR stated that the Chinese government viewed trade secret cases as routine commercial disputes, rather than as serious violations of the law. It further said that even though the Chinese government had reported that it had completed its plan to require the use of legitimate software by government entities at the central and provincial level, U.S. software firms had reported only a modest increase in sales to the government.

Market access in China remains a significant problem for many U.S. IP industries (such as music and films) and is considered to be a significant cause of high IPR piracy rates. For example, until recently, China limited imports of foreign films to 20 per year. During the visit to the United States by then-Chinese Vice President Xi Jinping (February 13-17, 2012), China agreed that it would allow more American exports to China of 3D, IMAX, and similar enhanced format movies on favorable commercial terms; strengthen the opportunities to distribute films through private enterprises rather than the state film monopoly; and ensure fairer compensation levels for U.S. blockbuster films distributed by Chinese SOEs.[128]

Technology Transfer Issues

When China entered the WTO in 2001, it agreed that foreign firms would not be pressured by government entities to transfer technology to a Chinese partner as part of the cost of doing business in China. However, many U.S. firms argue that this is a common Chinese practice, although this is difficult to quantify because, oftentimes, U.S. business representatives appear to try to avoid negative publicity regarding the difficulties they encounter doing business in China out of concern over retaliation by the Chinese government.[129]

In 2011, then-U.S. Treasury Secretary Timothy Geithner charged that "we're seeing China continue to be very, very aggressive in a strategy they started several decades ago, which goes like this: you want to sell to our country, we want you to come produce here. If you want to come produce here, you need to transfer your technology to us." A 2012 AmCham China survey reported that 33% of its respondents stated that technology transfer requirements were negatively affecting their businesses.[130] A 2010 study by the U.S. Chamber of Commerce stated that growing pressure on foreign firms to share technology in exchange for market access in China was forcing such firms to "anguish over balancing today's profits with tomorrow's survival."[131]

However, a 2011 survey by the USCBC found that technology transfer requirements by Chinese entities (both government and private) did not rank among the top 10 challenges faced by the Council's members in 2010. Among U.S. firms where technology was an issue, when asked if their company had been asked to transfer technology to China over the past three years, 18% answered yes. Among the respondents that had been asked to transfer technology, 20% said the pressure came from a government entity, while 80% said that it came from a Chinese company.[132] Of the respondents who said they were asked to transfer technology, 40% stated that they found the requests acceptable, 30% refused the requests, 15% negotiated to mitigate the amount of technology transfer, and 10% said they had to transfer the technology requested in order to gain access to the Chinese market. As noted by the USCBC:

> The PRC [People's Republic of China] certainty has a long-term strategy to bring in foreign technology. But technology is not simply "given to China." Instead, technology is typically licensed to a China-based entity in which the foreign company has an ownership stake. In many cases the foreign company owns 100 percent of the entity in China; in some cases, the foreign company must form a joint venture with a Chinese partner. In exchange, the company determines a value of the technology to be transferred and negotiates a payment— the technology is rarely "given" for free.[133]

Press reports indicate that the USTR's office is currently seeking information from U.S. manufacturers on examples of efforts by the Chinese government to force the transfer of technology from U.S. companies operating in China. This issue was discussed during President Obama's meeting with then-Chinese Vice President Xi Jinping on February 14, 2012.[134] A White House Factsheet of the meeting stated: "China reiterates that technology transfer and technological cooperation shall be decided by businesses independently and will not be used by the Chinese government as a pre-condition for market access."

In the 112th Congress, S. 2063 (Webb) would have prohibited the transfer by a U.S. commercial entity of any proprietary technology or intellectual property that was researched, developed, or commercialized using a contract, grant, loan, loan guarantee, or other financial assistance provided or awarded by the U.S. government to certain foreign entities (such as those that are owned or controlled by a foreign government) unless the Secretary of

Commerce determined (and issued a waiver) that the transfer would not compromise the U.S. economic interests or competitiveness.

Cyber Security Issues

Cyber-attacks against U.S. firms have raised concerns over the potential large-scale theft of U.S. IPR and its economic implications for the United States. A 2011 report by McAfee (a U.S. global security technology company) stated that its investigation had identified targeted intrusions into more than 70 global companies and warned that "every conceivable industry with significant size and valuable intellectual property has been compromised (or will be shortly), with the great majority of the victims rarely discovering the intrusion or its impact."[135] Many U.S. analysts and policy makers contend that the Chinese government is a major source of cyber-economic espionage against U.S. firms. For example, Representative Mike Rogers, chairman of the House Permanent Select Committee on Intelligence, stated at an October 4, 2011, hearing that

> Attributing this espionage isn't easy, but talk to any private sector cyber analyst, and they will tell you there is little doubt that this is a massive campaign being conducted by the Chinese government. I don't believe that there is a precedent in history for such a massive and sustained intelligence effort by a government to blatantly steal commercial data and intellectual property. China's economic espionage has reached an intolerable level and I believe that the United States and our allies in Europe and Asia have an obligation to confront Beijing and demand that they put a stop to this piracy.[136]

According to a report by the U.S. Office of the Director of National Intelligence (DNI): "Chinese actors are the world's most active and persistent perpetrators of economic espionage. U.S. private sector firms and cyber security specialists have reported an onslaught of computer network intrusions that have originated in China, but the IC (Intelligence Community) cannot confirm who was responsible." The report goes on to warn that

> China will continue to be driven by its longstanding policy of "catching up fast and surpassing" Western powers. The growing interrelationships between Chinese and U.S. companies—such as the employment of Chinese-national technical experts at U.S. facilities and the off-shoring of U.S. production and R&D to facilities in China—will offer Chinese government agencies and businesses increasing opportunities to collect sensitive US economic information.[137]

On February 19, 2013, Mandiant, a U.S. information security company, issued a report documenting extensive economic cyber espionage by a Chinese unit (which it designated as APT1) with alleged links to the Chinese People's Liberation Army (PLA) against 141 firms, covering 20 industries, since 2006. The report stated:

> Our analysis has led us to conclude that APT1 is likely government-sponsored and one of the most persistent of China's cyber threat actors. We believe that APT1 is able to wage such a long-running and extensive cyber espionage campaign in large part because it receives direct government support. In seeking to identify the organization behind this activity, our research found that People's Liberation Army (PLA's) Unit 61398 is similar to APT1 in its mission, capabilities, and resources. PLA Unit 61398 is also located in precisely the same area from which APT1 activity appears to originate.[138]

On March 11, 2013, Tom Donilon, National Security Advisor to President Obama, stated in a speech that the United States and China should engage in a constructive dialogue to establish acceptable norms of behavior in cyberspace; that China should recognize the urgency and scope of the problem and the risks it poses to U.S. trade relations and the reputation to Chinese industry; and that China should take serious steps to investigate and stop cyber espionage.[139] Following a meeting with Chinese President Xi Jinping in June 2013, President Obama warned that if cyber security issues are not addressed and if there continues to be direct theft of United States property, then "this was going to be a very difficult problem in the economic relationship and was going to be an inhibitor to the relationship really reaching its full potential."

On May 7, 2013, Senator Levin introduced S. 884, the Deter Cyber Theft Act. The bill would require the Director of National Intelligence (DNI) to develop a watch list and a priority watch list (determined to engage in the most egregious economic or industrial espionage in cyberspace) of foreign countries that engage in economic or industrial espionage in cyberspace with respect to U.S. trade secrets or proprietary information. The bill would require the president to block import of products containing stolen U.S. technology; products made by state-owned enterprises of nations on the DNI's priority watch list that are similar to items identified in the DNI's report as stolen or targeted U.S. technology; or made by a company the DNI identifies as having benefited from theft of U.S. technology or proprietary information.[140]

China's Obligations in the World Trade Organization

Negotiations for China's accession to the General Agreement on Tariffs and Trade (GATT) and its successor organization, the WTO, began in 1986 and took over 15 years to complete. During the WTO negotiations, Chinese officials insisted that China was a developing country and should be allowed to enter under fairly lenient terms. The United States insisted that China could enter the WTO only if it substantially liberalized its trade regime. In the end, a compromise was reached that required China to make immediate and extensive reductions in various trade and investment barriers, while allowing it to maintain some level of protection (or a transitional period of protection) for certain sensitive sectors. China's WTO membership was formally approved at the WTO Ministerial Conference in Doha, Qatar, on November 10, 2001. On November 11, 2001, China notified the WTO that it had formally ratified the WTO agreements, and on December 11, 2001, it formally joined the WTO.[141]

Under the WTO accession agreement, China agreed to the following.

- Reduce the average tariff for industrial goods from 17% to 8.9%, and average tariffs on U.S. priority agricultural products from 31% to 14%.
- Limit subsidies for agricultural production to 8.5% of the value of farm output, eliminate export subsidies on agricultural exports, and notify the WTO of all government subsidies on a regular basis.
- Within three years of accession, grant full trade and distribution rights to foreign enterprises (with some exceptions, such as for certain agricultural products, minerals, and fuels).
- Provide nondiscriminatory treatment to all WTO members, such as treating foreign firms in China no less favorably than Chinese firms for trade purposes.
- End discriminatory trade policies against foreign invested firms in China, such as domestic content rules and technology transfer requirements.
- Implement the WTO's Trade-Related Aspects of Intellectual Property Rights (TRIPS) Agreement upon accession (which sets basic standards on IPR protection and rules for enforcement).
- Fully open the banking system to foreign financial institutions within five years (by the end of 2006).
- Allow joint ventures in insurance and telecommunication (with various degrees of foreign ownership allowed).

WTO Implementation Issues

Getting China into the WTO under a comprehensive trade liberalization agreement was a major U.S. trade objective during the late 1990s. Many U.S. policy makers at the time maintained that China's WTO membership would encourage the Chinese government to deepen market reforms, promote the rule of law, reduce the government's role in the economy, further integrate China into the world economy, and enable the United States to use the WTO's dispute resolution mechanism to address major trade issues. As a result, it was hoped, China would become a more reliable and stable U.S. trading partner. U.S. trade officials contend that in the first years after it joined the WTO, China made noteworthy progress in adopting economic reforms that facilitated its transition toward a market economy and increased its openness to trade and FDI. However, beginning in 2006, progress toward further market liberalization appeared to slow. By 2008, U.S. government and business officials noted evidence of trends toward a more restrictive trade regime.[142] The USTR's 12th annual report to China on WTO compliance (issued in December 2013) identified several areas of concern, including[143]

- Failure by the Chinese government to maintain an effective IPR enforcement regime;
- Industrial policies and national standards that attempt to promote Chinese firms (while discriminating against foreign firms);
- Restrictions on trading and distribution rights;
- Discriminatory and unpredictable health and safety rules on imports (especially agricultural products);
- Burdensome regulations and restrictions on services; and
- Failure to provide adequate transparency of trade laws and regulations.

As of January 2014, the United States has brought 14 dispute settlement cases against China, 9 of which have been resolved or ruled upon.[144] China has nine WTO cases against the United States as well.[145] The U.S. cases are summarized below.

Pending U.S. WTO Dispute Settlement Cases Against China
- On September 17, 2012, the USTR announced that it had initiated a WTO dispute settlement case against China over it export subsidies to auto and auto parts manufacturers in China.[146]

- On March 13, 2012, the United States, Japan, and the European Union jointly initiated a dispute settlement case against China's restrictive export policies (such as quotas, tariffs, and minimum export prices) on rare earths and two other minerals.[147]
- On September 15, 2010, the USTR's office announced it was bringing a WTO case against China over its improper application of antidumping duties and countervailing duties on imports of grain oriented flat-rolled electrical steel from the United States. A WTO panel in June 2012 ruled largely in favor of the U.S. position and this was generally upheld by a WTO Appellate Body in October 2012. However, on December 24, 2013, the USTR stated that China had failed to bring its duties into compliance with WTO rules.

Resolved Cases or a WTO Panel Has Issued a Ruling[148]

- In May 2012, the United States initiated a WTO dispute settlement case China's improper use of anti-dumping and countervailing duties on broiler products. On August 5, 2013, the USTR announced that the United States had largely prevailed in the case.
- On September 15, 2010, the USTR's office announced it was bringing a WTO dispute settlement case against China over its discrimination against U.S. suppliers of electronic payment services (EPS). The United States charged that China permits only a Chinese entity (China Union Pay) to supply electronic payment services for payment card transactions denominated and paid in RMB in China, that service suppliers of other Members can only supply these services for payment card transactions paid in foreign currency, that China requires all payment card processing devices to be compatible with that entity's system and that payment cards must bear that company's logo, and that the Chinese entity has guaranteed access to all merchants in China that accept payment cards, while services suppliers of other WTO members must negotiate for access to merchants.[149] On July 16, 2012, the USTR announced that the United States had largely prevailed in the dispute.
- On June 23, 2009, the United States brought a case against China's export restrictions (such as export quotas and taxes) on raw materials (bauxite, coke, fluorspar, magnesium, manganese, silicon metal, silicon carbide, yellow phosphorus, and zinc). The United States charged that such policies are intended to lower prices for Chinese

firms (steel, aluminum, and chemical sectors) in order to help them obtain an unfair competitive advantage. China claims that these restraints are intended to conserve the environment and exhaustible natural resources. In July 2011, a WTO panel issued a report that China's export taxes and quotas on raw materials violated its WTO commitments. It further found that China failed to show that restrictions were linked to conservation of exhaustible natural resources for some of the raw materials or to protect the health of its citizens (by reducing pollution).[150] China appealed the WTO panel's ruling. However, on January 30, 2012, a WTO Appellate Body affirmed that China's export quotas and export taxes on certain raw materials violated its WTO commitments.[151] U.S. Trade Representative Ron Kirk called the decision a "tremendous victory for the United States," and said that it would ensure that "core manufacturing industries in this country can get the materials they need to produce and compete on a level playing field."[152]

- On December 22, 2010, the USTR's office announced that it would bring a WTO case against China over a government program that extended subsidies to Chinese wind power equipment manufacturers that use parts and components made in China rather than foreign-made parts and components. On June 7, 2011, the USTR's office announced that China had agreed to end these subsidies. However, the USTR noted that it had taken significant investigatory efforts by the U.S. government, working with industry and workers, to uncover China's wind subsidies because of the lack of transparency in China. The USTR further noted that, under the terms of China's WTO accession, it was required to fully report its subsidy programs to the WTO, which, to date, it has failed to do.[153]

- On December 19, 2008, the USTR filed a WTO case against China over its support for "Famous Chinese" brand programs, charging that such programs utilize various export subsidies (including cash grant rewards, preferential loans, research and development funding to develop new products, and payments to lower the cost of export credit insurance) at the central and local government level to promote the recognition and sale of Chinese brand products overseas. On December 18, 2009, the USTR announced that China had agreed to eliminate these programs.

- On March 3, 2008, the USTR requested WTO dispute resolution consultations with China regarding its discriminatory treatment of

U.S. suppliers of financial information services in China. On November 13, 2008, the USTR announced that China had agreed to eliminate discriminatory restrictions on how U.S. and other foreign suppliers of financial information services do business in China.

- On April 10, 2007, the USTR filed a WTO case against China, charging that it failed to comply with the TRIPS agreement (namely in terms of its enforcement of IPR laws). On January 26, 2009, the WTO ruled that many of China's IPR enforcement policies failed to fulfill its WTO obligations. On June 29, 2009, China announced that it would implement the WTO ruling by March 2010.
- On April 10, 2007, the USTR filed a WTO case against China charging that it failed to provide sufficient market access to IPR-related products, namely in terms of trading rights and distribution services. In August 2009, a WTO panel ruled that many of China's regulations on trading rights and distribution of films for theatrical release, DVDs, music, and books and journals were inconsistent with China's WTO obligation. China appealed the decision, but lost, and in February 2010 stated that it would implement the WTO's ruling.
- On February 5, 2007, the USTR announced it had requested WTO dispute consultations with China over government regulations that give illegal (WTO-inconsistent) import and export subsidies to various industries in China (such as steel, wood, and paper) that distort trade and discriminate against imports.[154] China's WTO accession agreement required it to immediately eliminate such subsidies. On November 29, 2007, China formally agreed to eliminate the subsidies in question by January 1, 2008.
- On March 30, 2006, the USTR initiated a WTO case against China over its use of discriminatory regulations on imported auto parts, which often applied the high tariff rate on finished autos (25%) to certain auto parts (which generally average 10%). The USTR charged that that the purpose of China's policy was to discourage domestic producers from using imported parts and to encourage foreign firms to move production to China. On February 13, 2008, a WTO panel ruled that China's discriminatory tariff policy was inconsistent with its WTO obligations (stating that the auto tariffs constituted an internal charge rather than ordinary customs duties, which violated WTO rules on national treatment). China appealed the decision, but a WTO Appellate Body largely upheld the WTO panel's decision.

- On March 18, 2004, the USTR announced it had filed a WTO dispute resolution case against China over its discriminatory tax treatment of imported semiconductors. The United States claimed that China applied a 17% value-added tax (VAT) on semiconductor chips that were designed and made outside China, but gave VAT rebates to domestic producers. Following consultations with the Chinese government, the USTR announced on July 8, 2004, that China agreed to end its preferential tax policy by April 2005. However, the USTR has expressed concern over new forms of financial assistance given by the Chinese government to its domestic semiconductor industry.

During his State of the Union Address in January 2012, President Obama announced plans to create a new Trade Enforcement Unit "charged with investigating unfair trade practices in countries like China." On February 28, 2012, President Obama issued an executive order establishing the Interagency Trade Enforcement Center within the USTR's office. Many analysts contend that the new enforcement unit could result in a sharp increase in the number of WTO dispute settlement cases brought by the United States against China.

China's Accession to the WTO Government Procurement Agreement (GPA)

Government procurement policies are largely exempt from WTO rules, except for those members which have signed the GPA.[155] When China joined the WTO, it indicated its intention to become a member of WTO's GPA as soon as possible, but, to date, has failed to submit an offer acceptable to current GPA members.

China's accession to the GPA is a major U.S. priority. China reports its annual government procurement spending at $179 billion (2011).[156] U.S. officials estimate this figure could be as high as $200 billion.[157] A study by the European Union Chamber of Commerce in China estimates that this figure could be well over $1 trillion if all levels of government are included, plus SOEs.[158] China currently maintains a number of restrictive government procurement practices and policies that favor domestic Chinese firms. Because of China's rapidly growing economy and significant infrastructure needs, China's accession to the GPA could result in significant new opportunities for U.S. firms.

China did not formally enter into negotiations to join the GPA until 2007, and its initial offer was deemed unacceptable by the other WTO GPA parties. China promised to revise its GPA offer, but did not do so until July 2010. That offer was deemed an improvement over the previous offer but was not accepted, in part because it excluded purchases by local and provincial governments as well as SOEs. A revised offer in December 2011 only covered public entities in three cities and two provinces.[159] Commenting on China's last offer, the USTR's office stated:

> China began its negotiations to join the GPA four years ago this month. Since that time, China has submitted three offers, each an improvement over the last. But China still has some distance to go before the procurement that it is offering is comparable to the extensive procurement that the United States and other Parties cover under the GPA. For example, we are urging China to cover state-owned enterprises, add more sub-central entities and services, reduce its thresholds for the size of covered contracts, and remove other broadexclusions.[160]

China submitted a new offer in November 2012. According to press reports, the U.S. representative to the WTO GPA committee stated that China's latest offer was "only another step but far from what we had expected." In particular, the United States and other GPA parties want China to improve its offer by including coverage of SOEs, lowering thresholds above which the GPA's nondiscrimination disciplines apply, removing several broad exclusions to coverage, and expanding coverage of sub-central entities. Some Members also stated opposition to China's proposal that it be allowed a five-year implementation period.[161] During the July 2013 S&ED talks, China pledged to submit a new revised GPA offer by the end of 2013 that would include lowering thresholds and increased coverage of sub-central entities.

Congressional concerns over China's restrictions on public procurement and failure to date to join the GPA resulted in the introduction of legislation in 112th Congress. H.R. 375 (Kildee) would have limited the total value of Chinese goods that could be procured by the U.S. government to the same value of U.S. goods procured by the Chinese government in the previous year, while H.R. 2271 (Royce) would have prohibited the federal government from awarding contracts to Chinese entities until China signs the GPA.

China's Currency Policy[162]

Unlike most advanced economies (such as the United States), China does not maintain a market-based floating exchange rate. Between 1994 and July 2005, China pegged its currency, the renminbi (RMB) or yuan, to the U.S.

dollar at about 8.28 yuan to the dollar.[163] In July 2005, China appreciated the RMB to the dollar by 2.1% and moved to a "managed float," based on a basket of major foreign currencies, including the U.S. dollar. In order to maintain a target rate of exchange with the dollar (and other currencies), the Chinese government has maintained restrictions and controls over capital transactions and has made large-scale purchases of U.S. dollars (and dollar assets).[164] According to the Bank of China, from July 2005 to July 2009, the official exchange rate went from 8.27 to 6.83 yuan per dollar, an appreciation of 21.1%.[165] However, once the effects of the global financial crisis became apparent, the Chinese government halted its appreciation of the RMB and subsequently kept the yuan/dollar exchange rate relatively constant at 6.83 from July 2009 to June 2010 in order to help limit the impact of the sharp decline in global demand for Chinese products. From June 19, 2010, (when appreciation was resumed) to December 17, 2013, the yuan/dollar exchange rate went from 6.83 to 6.11, an appreciation of 11.8%. Most of the appreciation occurred in 2010 and 2011. From January 1, 2012, to December 17, 2013, the RMB appreciated by only 3.6% against the dollar. Some analysts maintain that this is an indicator that the Chinese government is continuing to heavily intervene in currency markets to hold the down value of RMB relatively constant in the face of weak global demand for Chinese exports. Others argue that market forces are the main cause of the slow appreciation of the RMB, noting that China's current account surplus and accumulation of foreign exchange reserves have slowed considerably over the past few years which, it is argued, have lessened the need for the Chinese government to intervene in currency markets.

Many U.S. policy makers, labor groups, and business representatives of import-sensitive industries have charged that China's currency remains significantly undervalued against the dollar. They claim that this policy provides an indirect subsidy to Chinese exporters (which makes Chinese goods less expensive in the United States), while acting as a de facto tariff on U.S. goods imported into China (which makes them more expensive). They argue that this policy has particularly hurt several U.S. manufacturing sectors that are forced to compete against low-cost Chinese products and has led to significant job losses in the United States, especially in manufacturing. Critics further charge that China's currency policy has been a major factor in the size and growth of the U.S. trade deficit with China. Some Members of Congress contend that, given the current high rate of unemployment in the United States, Chinese "currency manipulation" can no longer be tolerated.

U.S. officials have urged China to continue efforts to rebalance its economy by boosting consumer demand (which would increase import demand) and decreasing the reliance on exports and fixed investment for economic growth. They argue that doing so would enable the Chinese government to move more quickly toward adopting a market-based exchange rate since the creation of new jobs in the nontrade sector would offset job losses in the trade sector resulting from an appreciation of the RMB.

Numerous bills have been introduced in Congress over the past few years that would seek to induce China to reform its currency policy or would attempt to address the perceived effects that policy has on the U.S. economy. For example, one bill in the 108th Congress would have imposed an additional duty of 27.5% on imported Chinese products unless China appreciated its currency to near market levels. In the 111th Congress, the House passed an amended version of H.R. 2378 (Tim Ryan), which would have made certain misaligned currencies (such as the RMB) actionable under U.S. countervailing duty cases on foreign government export subsidies (although the Senate did not take up the bill). In the 112th Congress, the Senate passed S. 1619, which would have provided for the identification of fundamentally misaligned currencies and required action to correct the misalignment for certain "priority" countries.

Two currency bills have been introduced in the 113th Congress: H.R. 1276 and S. 1114. H.R. 1276, the Currency Reform for Fair Trade Act was introduced by Representative Sander Levin on March 20, 2013. The bill is identical to the one he introduced in the 112th Congress (H.R. 639) and nearly identical to H.R. 2378, which passed the House during the 111th Congress by a vote of 284 to 123. The bill would seek to clarify certain provisions of U.S. countervailing duty laws (pertaining to foreign government export subsidies) that would allow the Commerce Department to consider a "fundamentally misaligned currency" as an actionable subsidy. S. 1114, the Currency Exchange Rate Oversight Reform Act of 2013, was introduced by Senator Sherrod Brown on June 7, 2013, and is essentially the same bill he introduced in 2011 and was passed by the Senate on October 11, 2011. The bill would provide for the identification of fundamentally misaligned currencies and require action to correct the misalignment for certain "priority" countries.

Some Members have expressed opposition to various currency bills aimed at China, arguing that they could violate U.S. obligations in the WTO. Other Members have argued that, while inducing China to adopt a market-based exchange rate is an important goal, the United States should give higher priority to addressing China's industrial policies and IPR infringement, which some view as more damaging to U.S. economic interests.

THE U.S.-CHINA STRATEGIC AND ECONOMIC DIALOGUE

On September 29, 2006, President George W. Bush and Chinese President Hu Jintao agreed to establish a Strategic Economic Dialogue (SED) to have discussions on major economic issues at the "highest official level." According to a U.S. Treasury Department press release, the intent of the SED was to "discuss long-term strategic challenges, rather than seeking immediate solutions to the issues of the day," in order to provide a stronger foundation for pursuing concrete results through existing bilateral economic dialogues.[166] The first meeting was held in December 2006. Four subsequent rounds of talks were held (the last was in December 2008).

While attending the G-20 summit in London on the global financial crisis on April 1, 2009, President Obama and Chinese President Hu agreed to continue the high-level forum, renaming it the U.S.-China Strategic and Economic Dialogue (S&ED). The new dialogue is based on two tracks. The first (the "Strategic Track") is headed by the Secretary of State on the U.S. side and focuses on political and strategic issues, while the second track (the "Economic Track") is headed by the U.S. Treasury Secretary on the U.S. side and focuses on financial and economic issues. Areas of discussion include economic and trade issues, counterterrorism, law enforcement, science and technology, education, culture, health, energy, the environment (including climate change), nonproliferation, and human rights.

One of the reported benefits of the U.S-China S&ED process is that it brings together top economic officials from both sides (as well as U.S. Cabinet officials and Chinese heads of ministries) on a regular basis, which enables both sides to identify their major positions and priorities on various issues and to develop long-term working relationships. Some in Congress have criticized the S&ED forum, arguing that it produces few concrete results, and that many of the results described in subsequent fact sheets that are jointly issued simply restate agreements or pledges China has already made. Others counter that U.S. engagement with China occurs on multiple levels throughout the year and that the S&ED meetings are in part a cumulative result of this process.

The July 2009 Economic Track Session

The first round of the S&ED was held in Washington, DC, on July 27-28, 2009, and involved 12 U.S. Cabinet officials and agency heads and 15 Chinese ministers, vice ministers, and agency heads. The session was focused heavily on issues relating to the global economic crisis. Then-Secretary of the Treasury Timothy Geithner stated: "Recognizing that cooperation between China and the United States will remain vital not only to the well-being of our two nations but also the health of the global economy, we agreed to undertake policies to bring about sustainable, balanced global growth once economic recovery is firmly in place."

The two sides agreed to establish a framework of cooperation based on four pillars:

- Advancing macroeconomic and structural policies to achieve sustainable and balanced growth;
- Promoting more resilient, open, and market-oriented financial systems;
- Strengthening trade and investment ties; and
- Strengthening the international financial architecture.

These pillars appear to have been aimed at deepening bilateral cooperation in response to the global economic crisis, continuing commitments on both sides to promote policies that seek to achieve more balanced economic growth, encouraging China to continue economic and financial reforms, expanding China's role and/or participation in international economic forums,[167] and attempting to avoid new forms of trade protection.

May 2010 Economic Track Session

The May 24-25, 2010, S&ED economic session focused heavily on the continuing efforts relating to the four pillars identified in the July 2009 session. Although few concrete accomplishments were announced at the end of the meetings, the two agreed to intensify talks on a number of bilateral economic and trade issues. The two sides pledged to

- Sign a cooperation protocol on small and medium-sized firms (SMEs);
- Boost economic cooperation at the central and local government level, such as promoting the establishment of state-to-province and city-to-city partnerships;
- Conduct "intensive expert and high-level discussions" as early as the summer of 2010 on innovation issues (such as China's indigenous

innovation proposals) and take into account the results of these talks in formulating and implementing their innovation measures;[168]
- Improve cooperation to address health and safety issues relating to U.S. sales of soybeans to China;
- Establish a cooperative mechanism between the U.S. Export-Import Bank and the Export-Import Bank of China on trade finance, and develop initiatives to promote exports by SMEs;
- Explore the possibility of cooperating to enable the United States to treat China as a market economy, and treat certain Chinese firms as market-oriented industries, for the purpose of U.S. trade remedy laws; and
- Boost investment opportunities and transparency.[169]

The May 2011 Economic Track

The third round of the S&ED was held in Washington, DC, on May 9-10, 2011. Prior to the meeting, U.S. officials identified several goals for the economic track of the S&ED, including ensuring that China followed through on previous economic and trade commitments (such as on IPR protection and indigenous innovation policies) and encouraging China to make a number of reforms to its financial sector (such as adopting market-based interest rates on bank deposits and expanding market access in China for U.S. financial firms). China pledged to continue to promote domestic consumption, improve IPR enforcement, eliminate all of its indigenous innovation products catalogues, improve transparency of its economic and trade policies, and provide significant new opportunities for U.S. financial services firms in China.

The May 2012 Economic Track

The fourth S&ED round was held in Beijing on May 3 and 4, 2012, and focused largely on economic rebalancing and boosting foreign access to China's financial services sector.[170] China pledged that it would:

- Increase the number of SOEs that pay dividends;
- Participate in negotiations (beginning in the summer of 2012) for new rules on official export financing with the United States and other major exporters;

- Provide nondiscriminatory treatment to all enterprises, regardless of type of ownership, in terms of credit, taxation, and regulatory policies so that U.S. firms can more easily compete against Chinese SOEs;
- Submit a new robust offer in 2012 to join the WTO's GPA and to intensify efforts to negotiate a BIT with the United States;
- Open up more sectors to FDI and improve the transparency of its investment approval process;
- Prioritize the protection of trade secrets, extend efforts to promote the use of legal software by Chinese enterprises, treat IPR owned or developed in other countries the same as IPR owned or developed in China, and hold discussions with U.S. officials on the implementation of China's commitment not to make technology transfer a precondition for doing business in China;
- Take steps to raise household income and lower prices of consumer goods, such as cutting import tariffs, reducing taxes on services, and raising deposit rates; and
- Expand market access to domestic financial markets by boosting the permitted level of foreign investment in its stock and bond markets, raising the permitted foreign equity stake in domestic securities joint ventures from 33% to 49%, and allowing foreign investors to establish joint venture brokerages to trade commodity and financial futures (with up to a 49% equity stake).

The May 2013 Economic Track

The 5th round of the S&ED talks were held in Washington, DC, on July 10-11, 2013. China pledged that it would:

- Negotiate a high-standard bilateral investment treaty with the United States that would include all stages of investment and all sectors based on a negative list approach;
- Submit a new and improved offer to join the WTO GPA by the end of 2013 that would include lowered thresholds and increased coverage of sub-central entities;
- Establish a pilot Free Trade Zone program in Shanghai which would enable foreign enterprises to compete on the same terms as Chinese firms across a wide range of services sectors;

- Affirmed its support for concluding negotiations by 2014 for new comprehensive international agreement setting guidelines on export financing by the major providers of export credits that would be consistent with international best practices;
- Eliminate preferential input pricing for energy, land, and water given to SOEs and develop a market-based mechanism for determining;
- Strengthening financial regulatory cooperation; and
- Continue to implement polices to boost private consumption such as raising social security and employment spending by two percentage points of total fiscal spending by the end of 2015.

Some analysts have argued that the S&ED structure should be reformed. For example, a report by the Center for Strategic and International Studies (CSIS) argues that ceremony has come to overwhelm substance in the S&ED, that pressure for short-term deliverables at each event has detracted from the dialogue's objective of fostering long-term strategic cooperation, and that the structure of the S&ED has undermined the efforts of individual agencies to work on critical elements of the relationship.[171] Others have complained about the lack of benchmarks in the S&ED process to evaluate outcomes of China's commitments. Others complain that the S&ED process often fails to achieve results on major issues. For example, at the July 2013 S&ED, China made no specific commitment on halting cyber theft.

CONCLUDING OBSERVATIONS

China's rapid economic growth and emergence as a major economic power have given China's leadership increased confidence in its economic model. The key challenges for the United States are to convince China that (1) it has a stake in maintaining the international trading system, which is largely responsible for its economic rise, and to take a more active leadership role in maintaining that system; and (2) further economic and trade reforms are the surest way for China to expand and modernize its economy. For example, by boosting domestic spending and allowing its currency to appreciate, China would likely import more, which would help speed economic recovery in other countries, promote more stable and balanced economic growth in China, and lessen trade protectionist pressures around the world. Improving IPR protection in China and providing nondiscriminatory treatment to foreign IP firms would likely foster greater innovation in China and attract more FDI in high technology than has occurred under current policies. Lowering trade barriers on imports would increase competition in China, lower costs for consumers, and boost economic efficiency. Some observers contend that reformist-minded officials in China will continue to push for greater free-market reforms, while others argue that vested interests in China (such as SOEs and export-oriented firms) who benefit from the status-quo will make further economic reforms more difficult to realize.

There are a number of views in the United States over how to more effectively address commercial disputes with China:

- Take a more aggressive stand against China, such as increasing the number of dispute settlement cases brought against China in the WTO, threatening to impose trade sanctions against China unless it addresses policies (such as IPR theft) that hurt U.S. economic interests, and making greater use of U.S. trade remedy laws (such as anti-dumping and countervailing measures) to address China's "unfair" trade practices.
- Intensify negotiations through existing high-level bilateral dialogues, such as the U.S.-China S&ED, which was established to discuss long-term challenges in the relationship. In addition, seek to complete ongoing U.S. negotiations with China to reach a high-standard BIT, as well as to finalize negotiations in the WTO toward achieving China's accession to the GPA. Continue to encourage China to implement comprehensive economic reforms, such as diminishing the role of the state in the economy and implementing policies to boost domestic consumption.
- Encourage China to join the Trans-Pacific Partnership (TPP) negotiations and/or seek to negotiate a bilateral a free trade agreement (FTA) with China that would require it to significantly improve IPR protection, lower trade and FDI barriers, and adopt new disciplines on the treatment of SOEs.[172]

End Notes

[1] This report focuses primarily on U.S.-China trade relations. For information on China's economy, see CRS Report RL33534, *China's Economic Rise: History, Trends, Challenges, and Implications for the United States*, by Wayne M. Morrison. For general information on U.S.-China political ties, see CRS Report R41108, *U.S.-China Relations: An Overview of Policy Issues*, by Susan V. Lawrence.

[2] The United States suspended China's MFN status in 1951, which cut off most bilateral trade. China's MFN status was conditionally restored in 1980 under the provisions set forth under Title IV of the 1974 Trade Act, as amended (including the Jackson-Vanik freedom-of-emigration provisions). China's MFN status (which was re-designated under U.S. trade law as "normal trade relations" status, or NTR) was renewed on an annual basis until January 2002, when permanent NTR was extended to China (after it joined the WTO in December 2001).

[3] U.S.-China Business Council, *China's WTO Compliance*, September 20, 2013.

[4] *OECD/WTO Trade in value-Added (TIVA) Database: China*, at http://www.oecd.org/sti/ind/TiVA%20China.pdf.

[5] U.S. Bureau of Economic Analysis, *U.S. International Services*.

[6] China's real GDP growth from 2008 to 2012 averaged 9.2%.

[7] Boston Consulting Group, *Big Prizes in Small Places: China's Rapidly Multiplying Pockets of Growth*, November 2010, p. 10.

[8] Boston Consulting Group, *Global Wealth 2013: Maintaining Momentum in a Complex World*, May 30, 2013.

[9] Source: *Economist Intelligence Unit*.

[10] China Daily, "China to invest 7t Yuan for Urban Infrastructure in 2011-15," May 13, 2013.

[11] China Daily, "China's Mobile Phone Users Hit 1.22 Billion," November 21, 2013.

[12] Boeing Corporation, *Current Market Outlook: 2013-2032*, September 5, 2013, available at http://www.boeing.com/assets/pdf/commercial/cmo/pdf/Boeing_Current_Market_Outlook_2013.pdf.

[13] Internet World Stats, at http://www.internetworldstats.com/stats.htm.

[14] A large share of these vehicles was produced by GM and its joint-venture partners in China. According to GM's website, it currently has 12 joint ventures and two wholly owned foreign enterprises in China and employees more than 58,000 workers. See, https://media.gm.com/media/cn/en/gm/company.html.

[15] BEA, *U.S. International Services*.

[16] Pacific Rim countries include Australia, Brunei, Cambodia, China, Hong Kong, Indonesia, Japan, South Korea, Laos, Macao, Malaysia, New Zealand, North Korea, Papua New Guinea, the Philippines, Singapore, Taiwan, Thailand, Vietnam, and several small island nations.

[17] China's accession to the WTO (with the reduction of trade and investment barriers) appears to have been a major factor behind the migration of computer production from other countries to China.

[18] USITC, *How Much of Chinese Exports Is Really Made In China? Assessing Foreign and Domestic Value-Added in Gross Exports*, report number 2008-03-B, March 2008, p. 21.

[19] Communications of the ACM, *Who Captures Value in a Global Innovation Network? The Case of Apple's iPod*, March 2009.

[20] U.S. data on FDI flows to and from China differ from Chinese data on FDI flows to and from the United States. This section examines only U.S. data.

[21] Investment is often a major factor behind trade flows. Firms that invest overseas often import machinery, parts, and other inputs from the parent company to manufacture products for export or sale locally. Other such invested overseas firms may produce inputs and ship them to their parent company for final production.

[22] 15 CFRS 806.15(a)(1). The 10% ownership share is the threshold considered to represent an effective voice or lasting influence in the management of an enterprise. See BEA, *International Economic Accounts, BEA Series Definitions*, available at http://www.bea.gov/international.

[23] BEA also reports FDI data according to broad industrial sections, including mining; utilities; wholesale trade; information; depository institutions; finance (excluding depository institutions); professional, scientific, and technical services; nonbank holding companies; manufacturing (including food, chemicals, primary and fabricated metals, machinery,

computers and electronic products, electrical equipment, appliances and components, transportation equipment, and other manufacturing); and other industries.

[24] For additional information on this issue, see CRS Report RL34314, *China's Holdings of U.S. Securities: Implications for the U.S. Economy*, by Wayne M. Morrison and Marc Labonte.

[25] The Treasury Department estimates that 72% of China's total holdings of U.S. government and private securities as of June 2012 were in U.S. Treasury securities.

[26] China's large annual trade surpluses and inflows of FDI are major contributors to China's accumulation of foreign exchange reserves, which totaled $3.4 trillion as of March 2013.

[27] However, over the past years, Chinese officials have expressed concern over the "safety" of their large holdings of U.S. debt. They worry that growing U.S. government debt and expansive monetary policies will eventually spark inflation in the United States, resulting in a sharp depreciation of the dollar. This would diminish the value of China's dollar asset holdings.[27] Some Chinese officials have called for replacing the dollar as the world's major reserve currency with some other currency arrangement, such as through the International Monetary Fund's special drawing rights system, although many economists question whether this would be a feasible alternative in the short run.

[28] China's holdings as of June 2012 were down $135 billion over June 2011 levels. In June 2012, Japan overtook China as the largest holder of U.S. public and private securities.

[29] Some observers characterize foreign holdings of U.S. Treasury securities as "foreign ownership of U.S. government debt."

[30] Office of the Secretary of Defense, *Report to Congress, Assessment of the National Security Risks Posed to the United States as a Result of the U.S. Federal Debt Owed to China as a Creditor of the U.S. Government*, July 2012.

[31] Note, U.S. and Chinese data on FDI flows between each other differ.

[32] According the BEA, direct investment implies that a person in one country has a lasting interest in, and a degree of influence over the management of, a business enterprise in another. As such, it defines FDI as ownership or control of 10% or more of an enterprise's voting securities, or the equivalent, is considered evidence of such a lasting interest or degree of influence over management.

[33] Chinese data lists the United States as the fourth-largest overall source of cumulative FDI through 2012. Chinese data on FDI flows with the United States differ from U.S. data.

[34] BEA data indicate that a significant cause of the decline in the stock of U.S. FDI in China over the past two years was from a decrease in the stock of U.S. FDI in depository institutions in China.

[35] BEA, *U.S. Direct Investment Abroad: Financial and Operating Data for U.S. Multinational Companies*, available at http://www.bea.gov/international/di1usdop.htm.

[36] Rhodium Group, *China Investment Monitor, Tracking Chinese Direct Investment in the U.S.* at http://rhgroup.net/ interactive/china-investment-monitor.

[37] Suntech press release, March 12, 2013, available at http://ir.suntech-power.com/phoenix.zhtml?c=192654&p=irol-newsArticle&id=1794801.

[38] Sany America website at http://www.sanyamerica.com/about-sany-america.php#ribbon.

[39] *Washington Post*, "Job creation seen as key to China's investment in U.S," January 19, 2011, available at http://www.washingtonpost.com/wp-dyn/content/article/2011/01/18/AR2011011806676.html.

[40] The purchase reportedly represents China's biggest single investment in the global auto parts-making industry and will make the Chinese company the largest private employer in Saginaw, Michigan at nearly 3,000 (source: New York Times, *G.M. Sells Parts Maker to a Chinese Company*, November 29, 2010). The firm owns 20 manufacturing plants worldwide, 5 regional engineering and test centers, and 14 local customer support centers.

[41] Xinhua News Agency, "U.S official hails Chinese Project in Texas, October 11, 2011."

[42] http://www.prnewswire.com/news-releases/huawei-poised-to-sustain-tens-of-thousands-of-job-opportunities-for-us-businesses-139525078.html.

[43] U.S. Department of the Treasury, *Preliminary Report on Foreign Portfolio Holdings of U.S. Securities at End-June 2011*, February, 29, 2012.

[44] For more information on the CIC, see CRS Report R41441, *China's Sovereign Wealth Fund: Developments and Policy Implications*, by Michael F. Martin.

[45] According to the BEA, Chinese majority-owned nonbank affiliates in the United States employed 1,700 U.S. workers in 2006 (most recent data available).

[46] During the 1980s, Japanese firms significantly boosted their FDI in the United States, such as in automobile manufacturing, in part to help to alleviate bilateral trade tensions.

[47] According to the United Nation's Conference on Trade and Development, China became the third-largest source of FDI outflows in 2012 at $84 billion (up from being the sixth largest in 2011).

[48] The White House, *Joint Fact Sheet on Strengthening U.S.-China Economic Relations*, February 14, 2012.

[49] CFIUS is an interagency committee that serves the President in overseeing the national security implications of foreign investment in the U.S. economy. See CRS Report RL33388, *The Committee on Foreign Investment in the United States (CFIUS)*, by James K. Jackson.

[50] Some argued, for example, that, given the relatively poor food safety record of many Chinese firms in China, the acquisition of Smithfield by Chinese investors could undermine food safety in the United States, and some suggested that the acquisition would eventually result in Chinese pork exports to the United States.

[51] The text of the letter can be found at http://www.stabenow.senate.gov/?p=press_release&id=1061.

[52] Senate Committee on Agriculture, Nutrition, and Forestry, available at http://www.ag.senate.gov/hearings/smithfield-and-beyond.

[53] The text of the letter can be found at http://www.finance.senate.gov/newsroom/chairman/release/?id=22b5b74e-5477-4ff8-9346-b46e0e158738.

[54] The letter is available at http://delauro.house.gov/index.php?option=com_content&view=article&id=1328:delauro-warren-demand-answers-on-shuanghui-smithfield-foods-deal&catid=2:2012-press-releases&Itemid=21.

[55] A123 Systems, Press Release, January 29, 2013, available at http://www.a123systems.com/62ce67cf-68aa-4b23-8b12-b8b210af1a3c/media-room-2013-press-releases-detail.htm.

[56] Investigative Report on the U.S. National Security Issues Posed by Chinese Telecommunications Companies Huawei and ZTE, A Report by Chairman Mike Rogers and Ranking Member C.A. Dutch Ruppersberger of the Permanent Select Committee on Intelligence, October 22, 2012, available at http://intelligence.house.gov/sites/intelligence.house.gov/files/documents/Huawei-ZTE%20Investigative%20Report%20(FINAL).pdf.

[57] New York Times, *Obama Orders Chinese Company to End Investment at Sites Near Drone Base*, September 28, 2012. Available at http://www.nytimes.com/2012/09/29/us/politics/chinese-company-ordered-to-give-up-stake-in-wind-farms-near-navy-base.html.

[58] Senator Robert Casey, *Press Release*, May 10, 2012, available at http://www.federalreserve.gov.

[59] The letter is available at http://www.casey.senate.gov/newsroom/press/release/?id=b940fb00-0a69-42d6-bcff-6ac72c8ce0c1.

[60] The letter also raised concerns over allegations that Huawei had ties to the Iranian government, had received substantial subsidies from the Chinese government, and had a poor record of protecting intellectual property rights.

[61] Huawei initially stated that it would decline CFIUS's recommendation with the intent of going through all of the procedures of the CFIUS process (including a potential decision by the President) in order to "reveal the truth about Huawei."

[62] Huawei, Open Letter, February 25, 2011, available at http://www.huawei.com/huawei_open_letter.do.

[63] A press release by Ansteel stated that its intensions are "to capitalize on the opportunity to enter into an overseas joint venture with a company that is focused on utilizing advanced

[64] technology in an environmentally friendly and highly profitable manner." See, http://www.steeldevelopment.com/documents/ansteel2010.pdf.

[64] See letter at http://visclosky.house.gov/SC_Geithner_CFIUS_7.2.10.pdf.

[65] Testimony of Rep. Peter J. Visclosky before the U.S.-China Economic and Security Review Commission on China's State-Owned and State-Controlled Enterprises, February 15, 2012.

[66] Emcore Press Release, June 28, 2010, available at http://www.emcore.com/news_events/release?y=2010&news=249.

[67] *New York Times*, "Chinese Withdraw Offer for Nevada Gold Concern," December 21, 2009.

[68] Although Huawei states that it is a private company wholly owned by its employees, many analysts contend that the company has close connections to the Chinese military. In addition, Huawei has also reportedly received extensive financial support from the Chinese government, including a $30 billion line of credit from China Development Bank.

[69] The Senate report of its version of FINSA (S.Rept. 110-80, S. 1610) noted that CNOOC's attempt to acquire UNOCAL "led many members of Congress to raise questions about the transfer of ownership or control of certain sectors of the U.S. economy to foreign companies, especially to foreign companies located within or controlled by countries the governments of which might not be sympathetic to U.S. regional security interests."

[70] IBM and Lenovo reportedly agreed to address national security concerns by CFIUS. For example, it was agreed that 1,900 employees from a North Carolina research facility, which IBM had shared with other technology companies, would move to another building. See the *Financial Times*, "US State Department limits use of Chinese PCs," May 18, 2006.

[71] U.S.-China Business Council, China's WTO Compliance, September 20, 2013.

[72] OECD, FDI Regulatory Restrictiveness Index, at http://www.oecd.org/investment/fdiindex.htm.

[73] The automotive industry was designated a "pillar industry" by the Chinese government in 1991.

[74] China also maintains a permitted category which represents a neutral position by the government that FDI in that area is neither encouraged nor discouraged. Prior to 2012, FDI in the manufacture of complete automobiles was listed as an encouraged category, but now is listed under the neutral category.

[75] One major function of the Guideline Catalogue for Foreign Investment is to promote FDI in sectors that the government has targeted for growth in its five-year macro-economic plans.

[76] USTR, 2011 *Report to Congress on China's WTO Compliance*, December 2011, p. 7.

[77] AmCham *China, China Business Climate Survey*, 2013, p. 9.

[78] For example, in March 2011, Senators Casey, Schumer, Stabenow, and Whitehouse sent a letter to the Obama Administration urging that they oppose Chinese mining projects in the United States because of China's restrictive and anticompetitive policies on rare earth. The letter noted China's prohibition on foreign investment in rare earth mining and requirements that FDI in rare earth smelting and separation can only be in the form of a joint venture. See http://www.casey.senate.gov/newsroom/press/release/print.cfm?id=81a1fa95-49d2-47a7-98b4-65973ae14ddc.

[79] *Inside U.S.-China Trade*, April 28, 2010.

[80] The Administration began efforts to review and revise the U.S. BIT model in 2009. The previous BIT model dated to 2004. The Administration's review process likely meant that negotiations with China for a BIT were someone limited.

[81] U.S. Department of the Treasury, *Remarks of Treasury Secretary Jacob J. Lew at the Close of the Fifth U.S.-China Strategic and Economic Dialogue*, July 13, 2013.

[82] The impact of globalization has been a controversial topic in the United States. Some argue that it has made it easier for U.S. firms to shift production overseas, resulting in lost jobs in the United States (especially in manufacturing) and lower wages for U.S. workers. Others contend that globalization has induced U.S. firms to become more efficient and to focus a greater share of their domestic manufacturing on higher-end or more technologically advanced production (while sourcing lower-end production abroad), making such firms

more globally competitive. The result has been that the United States continues to be a major global manufacturer in terms of value-added, but there are fewer U.S. workers in manufacturing.

[83] World Trade Organization, *Trade Policy Review Body, Trade Policy Review, Report by the Secretariat, China*, Revision, 2010, Part 2, p. 1.

[84] U.S. Trade Representative, *2013 USTR Report to Congress on China's WTO Compliance*, December 2013, p. 2.

[85] U.S.-China Economic and Security Review Commission, *An Analysis of State-owned Enterprises and State Capitalism in China*, by Andrew Szamosszegi and Cole Kyle, October 26, 2011, p.1.

[86] *Xinhua Agency*, October 24, 2012.

[87] Xinhua News Agency, October 24, 2010.

[88] Testimony for the U.S.–China Economic and Security Review Commission by Derek Scissors, Ph.D, *Chinese State Owned Enterprises and the US Policy on China*, February 12, 2012.

[89] Anderson, G.E., PhD, *Designated Drivers, How China Plans to Dominate the Global Auto Industry*, 2012, p. 2.

[90] Lund University, *Lending for Growth? An Analysis of State-Owned Banks in China*, by Fredrik N.G. Anderson, Katarzyna Burzynska, and Sonja Opper, June 2013, p. 41.

[91] The Economist, *State Capitalism's Global Reach, New Masters of the Universe, How State Enterprise is Spreading*, January 21, 2012.

[92] Lund University, *Lending for Growth? An Analysis of State-Owned Banks in China*, by Fredrik N.G. Anderson, Katarzyna Burzynska, and Sonja Opper, June 2013, p. 41.

[93] McGregor, Richard, *The Party, the Secret World of China's Communist Rulers*, 2010, p. 204.

[94] As some observers describe it, China wants to go from a model of "made in China" to "innovated in China."

[95] The MLP identifies main areas and priority topics, including energy, water and mineral resources, the environment, agriculture, manufacturing, communications and transport, information industry and modern service industries, population and health, urbanization and urban development, public security, and national defense. The report also identifies 16 major special projects and 8 "pioneer technologies."

[96] *R&D Magazine*, December 22, 2009.

[97] U.S. business representatives also claim that the Chinese government is using tax incentives, standards setting and requirements, security regulations, subsidies, technology transfer requirements, and other measures to promote the goals of indigenous innovation.

[98] AmCham China, *2011 White Paper*, April 26, 2011, p. 66.

[99] A copy of the letter can be found at http://online.wsj.com/public/resources/documents/chinaprocurementletter1210.pdf.

[100] Some U.S. business representatives argue that one of the main goals of China's indigenous innovation regulations is to induce foreign firms to boost their R&D activities in China in order to qualify for government contracts.

[101] Transitional Review Under Section 18 of the Protocol on the Accession of the People's Republic of China, Report to the General Council by the Chair, November 17, 2011, p. 4.

[102] Wall Street Journal, *China Defends Rule On 'Indigenous' Tech*, December 15, 2009.

[103] The White House, *U.S. - China Joint Statement*, January 19, 2011.

[104] According to a U.S. fact sheet on the meeting "China pledged to eliminate all of its government procurement indigenous innovation products catalogues and revise Article 9 of the draft Government Procurement Law Implementing Regulations (which have preferences in government procurement to national indigenous innovation products), in fulfillment of President Hu's January 2011 commitment not to link Chinese innovation policies to government procurement preferences. See U.S. Department of the Treasury, The 2011 U.S.-China Strategic and Economic Dialogue U.S. Fact Sheet – Economic Track, May 10, 2011.

[105] U.S. Department of Commerce, *22nd U.S.-China Joint Commission on Commerce and Trade Fact Sheet*, November 21, 2011.

[106] U.S.-China Business Council, *Status Report: China's Innovation and Government Procurement Policies*, May 1, 2013, at https://www.uschina.org/files/public/documents/2013/05/innovation-status-report.pdf.

[107] U.S.-China Business Council, USCBC 2012 China Business Environment Survey Results: Continued Growth and Profitability; Tempered Optimism Due to Rising Costs, Competition, and Market Barriers, October 2012, p. 6, available at https://www.uschina.org/info/members-survey/2012/pdfs/uscbc-2012-member-survey-results.pdf.

[108] Foreign Affairs, *China's Innovation Wall: Beijing's Push for Homegrown Technology*, September 28, 2010.

[109] U.S. Chamber of Commerce, *China's Drive for 'Indigenous Innovation' - A Web of Industrial Policies*, February 2011, p. 4.

[110] USITC, China: Intellectual Property Infringement, Indigenous Innovation Policies, and Frameworks for Measuring the Effects on the U.S. Economy (Investigation No. 332-514, USITC Publication 4199, November 2010, pp. 6-7.

[111] See CRS Report RL34292, *Intellectual Property Rights and International Trade*, by Shayerah Ilias Akhtar and Ian F. Fergusson.

[112] U.S. Department of Commerce, *Intellectual Property and the U.S. Economy: Industries in Focus*, March 2012, available at http://www.esa.doc.gov/sites/default/files/reports/documents/ipandtheuseconomyindustriesinfocus.pdf.

[113] Nam Pham, *The Impact of Innovation and the Role of Intellectual Property Rights on U.S. Productivity, Competitiveness, Jobs, Wages and Exports*, 2010, NDP Consulting.

[114] Communications of the ACM, *Who Captures Value in a Global Innovation Network? The Case of Apple's iPod*, March 2009.

[115] The Commission on the Theft of American Intellectual Property, *the Report of the Commission on the Theft of Intellectual Property*, May 2013.

[116] AmCham China, *China Business Climate Survey Report*, 2013, p. 11.

[117] The United States International Trade Commission, *China: Effects of Intellectual Property Infringement and Indigenous Innovation Policies on the U.S. Economy*, USITC Publication 4226, May 2011, p. xiv.

[118] BSA, *Shadow Market, 2011 BSA Global Software Piracy Study, Ninth Edition*, May 2012, at http://portal.bsa.org/ globalpiracy2011/downloads/study_pdf/2011_BSA_Piracy_Study-Standard.pdf.

[119] U.S. Customs and Border Protection, *Intellectual Property Rights, Fiscal Year 2012 Seizure Statistics*, February 2013, available at http://www.cbp.gov/linkhandler/cgov/trade/priority_trade/ipr/ipr_communications/seizure/fy2012_final_stats.ctt/fy2012_final_stats.pdf.

[120] Testimony of Jeremie Waterman, Senior Director, Greater China, U.S. Chamber of Commerce, before the U.S. International Trade Commission, *Hearing on China: Intellectual Property Infringement, Indigenous Innovation Policies, and Frameworks for Measuring the Effects on the U.S. Economy*, June 15, 2010.

[121] AMSC claims Sinovel had obtained the intellectual property from a former AMSC employee who was now under arrest in Austria for economic espionage and fraudulent manipulation of data.

[122] AMSC Press Release, "AMSC Filing Criminal and Civil Complaints Against Sinovel," September 14, 2011.

[123] AMSC, Press Release, April 10, 2012, at http://files.shareholder.com/downloads/AMSC/2346100399x0x558743/f01e0c5a-a526-4102-a818-f61f2d71ef79/AMSC_News_2012_4_10_Commercial.pdf.

[124] "Data Theft Case May Test U.S. China Ties," *Boston Globe*, September 19, 2011.

[125] The JCCT was established in 1983 to serve as a forum for high-level dialogue on major bilateral trade issues.

[126] USTR, *2012 Special 301 Report*, April 2012, available at http://www.ustr.gov/sites/default/files/ 2012%20Special%20301%20Report_0.pdf.

[127] USTR, *2013 Special 301 Report*, April 2013, available at http://www.ustr.gov/sites/default/files/ 05012013%202013%20Special%20301%20Report.pdf.
[128] The White House, *Press Release*, February 17, 2012, at http://www.whitehouse.gov/the-press-office/2012/02/17/ united-states-achieves-breakthrough-movies-dispute-china.
[129] China denies that public officials exert such pressure and that any technology transfers that do occur in China are the result of commercial agreements between companies.
[130] AmCham China, *2012 China Business Climate Survey Report*, March 2012, available at http://www.amchamchina.org/businessclimate2012.
[131] U.S. Chamber of Commerce, *China's Drive for 'Indigenous Innovation' - A Web of Industrial Policies,* July 29, 2010.
[132] However, the Council notes that since the Chinese government maintains approval authority for investment decisions, which may be used by Chinese firms as leverage when attempting to negotiate technology transfer agreements with U.S. firms.
[133] U.S.-China Business Council, *USCBC 2011 China Business Environment Survey Results: Market Growth Continues, Companies Expand, But Full Access Elusive for Many,* November 2011, p. 20.
[134] Inside Trade, *USTR Seeks Info From Manufacturers On Forced Technology Transfer To China,* January 31, 2012.
[135] The report did not identify China (or any country) as the source of the intrusions. McAfee, *Revealed: Operation Shady Rat, An Investigation of Targeted Intrusions Into More Than 70 Global Companies, Governments, and Nonprofit Organizations During the Last Five Years,* 2011.
[136] House Permanent Select Committee on Intelligence, *Chairman Mike Rogers Opening Statement at the Hearing on Cyber Threats and Ongoing Efforts to Protect the Nation,* October 4, 2011.
[137] DNI, Office of the National Counterintelligence Executive, *Foreign Spies Stealing U.S. Economic Secrets in Cyberspace, Report to Congress on Foreign Economic Collection and Industrial Espionage*: 2009-2011, October 2011.
[138] Mandiant, *APT1: Exposing One of China's Cyber, Espionage Units*, February 19, 2013, p. 2.
[139] U.S. Asia Society, Complete Transcript: Thomas Donilon at Asia Society, New York March 11, 2013.
[140] Office of Senator Carl Levin, Newsroom, Bipartisan Group of Senators Introduces Legislation to Combat Cyber Theft, May 7, 2013, at http://www.levin.senate.gov/newsroom/press/release/bipartisan-group-of-senators-introduces-legislation-to-combat-cyber-theft.
[141] Following China's WTO accession, the United States, in January 2002, granted China conditional basis) to ensure that the United States and China had a formal trade relationship under the rules of the WTO.
[142] China generally implemented its tariff reductions on schedule.
[143] USTR, *2013 Report to Congress on China's WTO Compliance*, December 2013.
[144] For an overview of the WTO's dispute settlement process, see CRS Report RS20088, *Dispute Settlement in the World Trade Organization (WTO): An Overview*, by Daniel T. Shedd, Brandon J. Murrill, and Jane M. Smith.
[145] The United States has been the largest target of China's dispute settlement cases in the WTO. Most of these cases have challenged certain U.S. applications of antidumping and countervailing measures.
[146] For additional information about this issue, see CRS Report R43071, *U.S.-Chinese Motor Vehicle Trade: Overview and Issues*, by Bill Canis and Wayne M. Morrison
[147] For additional information on China's restrictions on rare earths, see CRS Report R42510, *China's Rare Earth Industry and Export Regime: Economic and Trade Implications for the United States*, by Wayne M. Morrison and Rachel Y. Tang.
[148] Often, cases are resolved through consultations before a case goes to a panel.
[149] WTO, *Dispute Settlement—Certain Measures Affecting Electronic Payments, Current Status*, August 31, 2012.

[150] A summary of the WTO panel report can be found at http://www.wto.org/english/tratop_e/dispu_e/cases_e/ds394_e.htm#bkmk394r.
[151] The Appellate Body declared moot and of no legal effect the Panel's findings regarding China's export licensing requirements, minimum export price requirements, administration and allocation of export quotas, and fees and formalities in connection with exportation because of inadequacies in the complainants' panel requests involving these measures.
[152] USTR, *Press Release*, January 31, 2012.
[153] USTR *Press Release*, June 7, 2011, available at http://www.ustr.gov/about-us/press-office/press-releases/2011/june/china-ends-wind-power-equipment-subsidies-challenged.
[154] Some programs gave tax preferences, tariff exemptions, discounted loans, or other benefits to firms that met certain export performance requirements, while others gave tax breaks for purchasing Chinese-made equipment and accessories over imports.
[155] The GPA is a plurilateral agreement among 41 WTO members (including the United States, Japan, and the 27 members of the European Union) that effectively provides market access for various nondefense government procurement projects to signatories to the agreement. Each member of the Agreement submits lists of government entities and goods and services (with thresholds and limitations) that are open to bidding by firms of the other GPA members. WTO members that are not signatories to the GPA, including those that are GPA observers (such as China), do not enjoy any rights under the GPA. Nor are non-GPA signatories in the WTO generally obligated to provide access to their government procurement markets.
[156] Xinhua News Agency, June 29, 2012, at http://news.xinhuanet.com/english/china/2012-06/29/c_131685154.htm.
[157] Testimony of Karen Laney, Acting Director of Operations, U.S. International Trade Commission before the Subcommittee on Terrorism, Nonproliferation, and Trade, Committee on Foreign Affairs, on *China's Indigenous Innovation, Trade, and Investment Policies*, March 9, 2011.
[158] European Chamber of Commerce in China, Public Procurement in China: European Business Experiences Competing for Public Contracts in China, 2011, p. 15, at http://www.europeanchamber.com.cn/en/publications-public-procurement-study-european-business-experiences-competing-for-public-contracts-in-china.
[159] Inside U.S. Trade, December 8, 2011.
[160] USTR Press Release, December 2011.
[161] *Inside U.S. Trade*, December 12, 2012.
[162] For additional information on this issue, see CRS Report RS21625, *China's Currency Policy: An Analysis of the Economic Issues*, by Wayne M. Morrison and Marc Labonte.
[163] The official name of China's currency is the renminbi, which is denominated in units of yuan.
[164] Much of China's trade is believed to be in U.S. dollars (e.g., exporters are often paid in dollars). The central government requires firms to exchange most of their dollars for RMB.
[165] Calculated from Bank of China data using the official government "middle rate."
[166] U.S. Treasury Department, *Press Release*, December 15, 2006.
[167] The United States is seeking to broaden China's participation in international economic institutions in order to promote the goal of helping to make China a "responsible stakeholder" in the global economy. This implies that, since China greatly benefits from the global trading system and is a major global economy, it should shoulder a greater responsibility in maintaining and promoting that system (rather than just enjoying the benefits of that system.
[168] The United States also pledged that it would review Chinese concerns relating to U.S. restrictions on high technology exports to China resulting from the current U.S. export control regime.
[169] The United States pledged that it welcomed investment from China and confirmed that review of foreign investment by the Committee on Foreign Investment in the United States ensures the consistent and fair treatment of all foreign investment without prejudice to the place of

origin. China promised to revise its Catalogue Guiding Foreign Investment in Industries and encourage and expand areas open to foreign investment, including those relating to high-technology, energy, and the environment. China also pledged to streamline the process for investment approval.

[170] The session was somewhat overshadowed by events relating to Chinese human rights advocate Chen Guangcheng who had been temporarily sheltered at the U.S. embassy in Beijing prior to the session.

[171] CSIS, *Crafting Asia Economic Strategy in 2013*, January 28, 2013, at http://csis.org/publication/crafting-asia-economic-strategy-2013.

[172] The TPP is a proposed regional free trade agreement among 12 countries, including Australia, Brunei, Canada, Chile, Japan, Malaysia, Mexico, New Zealand, Peru, Singapore, the United States, and Vietnam.

In: China and the U.S.   ISBN: 978-1-63321-156-8
Editor: Arthur Santoni   © 2014 Nova Science Publishers, Inc.

Chapter 2

U.S.-CHINA TRADE: UNITED STATES HAS SECURED COMMITMENTS IN KEY BILATERAL DIALOGUES, BUT U.S. AGENCY REPORTING ON STATUS SHOULD BE IMPROVED[*]

United States Government Accountability Office

WHY GAO DID THIS STUDY

China is the largest destination for U.S. exports outside North America and also the source of the largest U.S. bilateral trade deficit. The countries engage in two high-level dialogues to address trade barriers and cross-cutting economic issues. These are the JCCT, co-led for the United States by Commerce and USTR, and the economic track of the S&ED, led by Treasury. GAO was asked to review China's bilateral trade commitments made in these dialogues. This report (1) describes trade and investment commitments China has made at the JCCT and S&ED; (2) describes U.S. agency tracking of China's implementation of these commitments; and (3) evaluates U.S. agency reporting on implementation. GAO analyzed documents, including public fact sheets stating commitments; interviewed officials, industry representatives,

---

[*] This is an edited, reformatted and augmented version of the United States Government Accountability Office publication, GAO-14-102, dated February 2014.

and other experts; used a structured process to categorize commitments; and reviewed reports officials identified as reporting implementation status of commitments.

WHAT GAO RECOMMENDS

To improve understanding of progress through the bilateral dialogues in increasing access to China's markets, USTR, in conjunction with Commerce and Treasury, should work to improve reporting on China's implementation of JCCT and S&ED trade and investment commitments. In written comments, USTR and Commerce did not directly agree or disagree with the recommendation, but raised several concerns. USTR maintained current reporting is comprehensive and Commerce noted resource constraints. GAO continues to believe improved reporting would benefit policymakers.

WHAT GAO FOUND

GAO identified 298 trade and investment commitments made by China in the U.S.-China Joint Commission on Commerce and Trade (JCCT)—184 since 2004—and the U.S.-China Strategic and Economic Dialogue (S&ED) and its predecessor—114 since 2007. The commitments range from affirmations of open trade principles to sector-specific actions. GAO identified 11 issue areas to characterize the content of each commitment. The prominence of issue areas, measured in number of commitments associated with an issue area, differs between the dialogues, reflecting differences in the dialogues' structure and focus. Intellectual property rights commitments are among those most common in the JCCT and investment commitments are among those most common in the S&ED. (For a detailed inventory of commitments and their categorization, see GAO-14-224SP.)

U.S. agencies track commitment implementation through several means, including outreach to domestic stakeholders, issue-based working groups with China in the JCCT, and consultations in advance of S&ED annual meetings. No single document is used to track implementation, according to U.S. officials. In addition, although there have been calls to use metrics such as exports and sales in developing commitments, agencies identified only one such commitment in the dialogues and cited challenges in identifying appropriate data.

Although several reports on trade barriers present information on JCCT and S&ED commitments, information on commitment implementation in these reports does not provide a clear and comprehensive picture of progress across the dialogues. The Office of the U.S. Trade Representative (USTR) produces these reports with assistance from other agencies, including the Departments of Commerce (Commerce) and Treasury (Treasury). GAO's analysis of 10 software commitments from 2008-2011 shows, for example, that the implementation status of most could not be clearly identified. More comprehensive reporting would give Congress and other policy makers a clearer understanding of progress and the role of the dialogues as they continue to assess challenges in the U.S.-China relationship.

ABBREVIATIONS

APEC	Asia-Pacific Economic Cooperation
Commerce	Department of Commerce
GPA	Government Procurement Agreement of the World Trade Organization
JCCT	U.S.-China Joint Commission on Commerce and Trade
NTE	National Trade Estimate Report on Foreign Trade Barriers
OSTP	Office of Science and Technology Policy
S&ED	U.S.-China Strategic and Economic Dialogue
SED	U.S.-China Strategic Economic Dialogue
State	Department of State
Treasury	Department of the Treasury
USDA	U.S. Department of Agriculture
USTR	Office of the U.S. Trade Representative
WTO	World Trade Organization

February 11, 2014

The Honorable Dana Rohrabacher
Chairman
Subcommittee on Europe, Eurasia, and Emerging Threats
Committee on Foreign Affairs
House of Representatives

The Honorable Frank Wolf
House of Representatives

The Honorable J. Randy Forbes
House of Representatives

Since China joined the World Trade Organization (WTO) in 2001, trade between the United States and China has grown substantially, with China now the largest destination for U.S. exports outside North America. However, U.S. imports from China exceed exports by more than $300 billion, making the U.S. trade deficit with China significantly larger than with any other trading partner. Despite actions by China to open its markets to the United States, formidable barriers remain. The governments of the United States and China are engaged in a number of forums that address trade issues, including two cabinet-level bilateral dialogues—the U.S.-China Joint Commission on Commerce and Trade (JCCT) and the U.S.-China Strategic and Economic Dialogue (S&ED).

The JCCT, initiated in 1983, focuses on addressing bilateral trade matters and promoting commercial opportunities. The S&ED, established in 2009, represents the highest-level bilateral dialogue to discuss a broad range of both strategic and economic issues. (The S&ED was preceded by the Strategic Economic Dialogue [SED] in 2006 through 2008.) Some observers and policy makers have raised questions about what commitments China has made and implemented as a result of these dialogues as well as what tangible benefits for the U.S. economy the dialogues have produced.

You asked us to review issues related to China's JCCT and S&ED trade and investment commitments. In this report, we (1) describe the commitments China made at the JCCT and the trade and investment commitments China made at the S&ED,[1] (2) describe U.S. agency tracking of China's implementation of these commitments, and (3) evaluate U.S. agency reporting on the status of commitment implementation.

To address these objectives, we analyzed documents and interviewed U.S. officials, industry representatives, and other experts. To describe the commitments, we analyzed public JCCT and S&ED fact sheets issued by the U.S. government to identify individual commitments made by China, including those made jointly with the United States, and categorized them by trade issue areas using a structured review process.[2] To describe U.S. agency tracking of commitment implementation, we obtained and analyzed documentary and testimonial evidence on relevant agency activities. To evaluate U.S. agency reporting on implementation status, we reviewed key reports that U.S. officials identified as containing their assessments of the implementation of commitments made in these dialogues, and discussed the results with officials and other experts. (Appendix I provides more detailed information on our scope and methodology.) In addition, an inventory of the commitments we identified and their categorization by issue area is provided in an online e- supplement, GAO-14-224SP.

We conducted this performance audit from May 2012 to February 2014 in accordance with generally accepted government auditing standards. Those standards require that we plan and perform the audit to obtain sufficient, appropriate evidence to provide a reasonable basis for our findings and conclusions based on our audit objectives. We believe that the evidence obtained provides a reasonable basis for our findings and conclusions based on our audit objectives.

BACKGROUND

Since 1979, when the United States and China signed a bilateral trade agreement, China's economy has grown at an unprecedented rate, as has China's bilateral economic engagement with the United States. In recent years, China's economy grew an average of 10 percent a year, and in 2010 China replaced Japan as the world's second largest economy. Total U.S.-China trade increased from $2 billion in 1979 to $536 billion in 2012. China is currently the second largest U.S. trading partner, the third largest U.S. export market, and the largest source of U.S. imports.

The governments of the United States and China have established two important bilateral dialogues—the JCCT and S&ED, which discuss and resolve trade and investment matters, including reducing trade barriers for U.S. firms and investors.[3] (See figure 1 for the organization of the JCCT and the S&ED.) According to senior U.S. officials, the United States also engages with China at all levels of government in other bilateral interactions, such as formal and informal conversations at U.S.-China summits. In addition, the two governments discuss trade and investment issues in multilateral forums, such as the WTO and the Asia-Pacific Economic Cooperation (APEC) forum.[4]

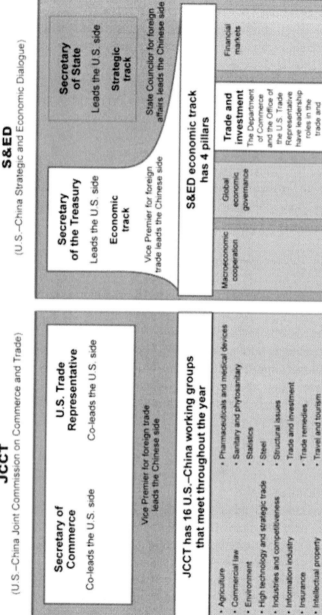

Source: GAO analysis of information from Commerce, USTR, Treasury, State, and USDA.

Note: On the U.S. side, the Department of Agriculture and the Office of the U.S. Trade Representative (USTR) co-chair the agriculture working group and the sanitary and phytosanitary working group, the Environmental Protection Agency and Commerce co-chair the environment working group, and Commerce and USTR chair or co-chair the remaining working groups.

Figure 1. U.S. Agency Roles in the JCCT and S&ED.

The JCCT, established in 1983, is the main bilateral dialogue for addressing trade matters and promoting commercial opportunities between the two countries. Since 2004, the U.S. Secretary of Commerce, the U.S. Trade Representative, and China's Vice Premier for foreign trade have co-chaired the JCCT.[5] The dialogue, which has multiple working groups focusing on specific issue areas, operates year-round and culminates in an annual plenary meeting that alternates between the United States and China. The two most recent JCCT plenary meetings took place in December 2012 in Washington, D.C., and in December 2013 in Beijing, China.

The S&ED, established by the Presidents of the United States and China in April 2009, represents the highest-level bilateral dialogue to discuss a broad range of issues between the two nations. The S&ED addresses bilateral, regional, and global economic and strategic issues, both medium and longer term. Under the S&ED, the two sides meet once a year, alternating between Washington, D.C., and Beijing. The fifth S&ED meeting was held in Washington, D.C., in July 2013. The S&ED has strategic and economic tracks; the U.S. Secretary of State and China's State Councilor for foreign affairs co-chair the strategic track, and the U.S. Treasury Secretary and China's Vice Premier for foreign trade co- chair the economic track. From 2006 through 2008, the S&ED was preceded by the SED, in which the two governments discussed the most important economic, but not political, issues in the bilateral relationship.

The S&ED's economic track has four pillars, one of which focuses on trade and investment,[6] and addresses short, medium, and longer term economic issues. In setting S&ED priorities, the Department of the Treasury (Treasury) and the National Security Staff lead an interagency process, working closely with the Department of Commerce (Commerce), the Office of the U.S. Trade Representative (USTR), and other agencies, on trade and investment issues. According to Treasury officials, discussions of S&ED economic track issues continue throughout the year between the annual plenary meetings.

Agencies report the outcomes of the JCCT and S&ED dialogues through public statements in the form of fact sheets that present commitments made by the United States and China. These fact sheets are issued following the conclusion of the JCCT and S&ED annual meetings. Commerce and USTR issue a JCCT fact sheet following the JCCT annual meeting; Treasury issues jointly with China an S&ED fact sheet for the economic track that presents the joint commitments negotiated by the United States and China following the S&ED annual meeting. Treasury also issues a U.S. fact sheet that discusses the benefits of the commitments for U.S. workers and companies. The Department of State (State) issues the fact sheet for the S&ED strategic track. According to senior U.S. agency officials, these fact sheets outline the official commitments negotiated with the Chinese government.

In addition to reporting commitments, the JCCT and S&ED fact sheets have in recent years included sections that identify cooperative or exchange activities between the United States and China.[7] (These are referred to as "cooperative activities" in JCCT fact sheets and "institutional arrangements" in S&ED fact sheets.) According to Commerce officials, JCCT cooperative activities are undertaken with the goal of advancing U.S. priorities and are often crucial for developing successful policy commitments from China. They may involve discussions with public and private sector participants focusing on issues or areas at the pre-commitment level. For example, in 2009, China and the United States held a program, pursuant to JCCT commitments, with public and private participants to discuss legal liability for intellectual property rights infringement that occurs on the Internet. There were JCCT commitments related to this issue in 2010 and 2012 that resulted, according to U.S. officials, in the Supreme People's Court's publication of a judicial interpretation stating that those who facilitate online infringement will be held jointly liable for that conduct. Similarly, the S&ED allows for activities, such as consultations or technical exchanges, that are separate from commitments but allow the two sides to engage in a dialogue on a range of issues. For example, in 2012 the United States and China agreed to expand technical exchanges under the U.S.-China Transportation Forum and enhance coordination under the APEC framework.

CHINA HAS MADE COMMITMENTS IN A NUMBER OF TRADE AND INVESTMENT AREAS AND SECTORS

China has made 298 trade and investment commitments since 2004 in the JCCT and S&ED, ranging from statements affirming open trade principles to statements that focus on trade actions specific to a sector.[8] The prominence of issue areas across the commitments differs between the dialogues, reflecting differences in the dialogues' structure and focus. Some commitments reaffirm prior commitments and some commitments acknowledge progress since the previous year's meeting.

Issue area	Number of JCCT commitments that include issue area	Number of S&ED commitments that include issue area
Government procurement	15	8
High technology trade	2	9
Innovation	11	10
Intellectual property rights	62	9
Investment	1	30
Multilateral issues	20	26
Open trade principles	0	7
Sector-specific issues	110	11
Technical and regulatory barriers to trade	45	14
Trade remedies	3	9
Transparency	19	24
Other	10	21

Sector	Number of JCCT commitments that include sector	Number of S&ED commitments that include sector
Agriculture	19	1
Distribution/retail	5	
Information technology and security	6	
Insurance	1	
New energy vehicles	3	
Pharmaceuticals and medical devices	28	
Postal/courier	3	
Shipping	1	
Software	18	4
Steel	1	
Telecommunications	12	
Textiles	1	
Transportation	3	5
Travel and tourism	6	1
Wind power	3	

JCCT U.S. – China Joint Commission on Commerce and Trade.

S&ED   U.S. – China Strategic and Economic Dialogue.
Source: GAO analysis of JCCT and S&ED fact sheets.
Note: We categorized commitments that did not fit the 11 issue areas as "other." We assigned up to three issue areas to each commitment because many commitments were related to more than one issue area. Thus, the numbers shown in this figure exceed the total number of commitments we identified for each dialogue, 184 commitments for the JCCT and 114 trade and investment commitments for the S&ED. See GAO-14-224SP for a full inventory of commitments and their categorization.

Figure 2. Issue Areas Identified within China's JCCT Commitments (2004-2012) and S&ED Trade and Investment Commitments (2007-2013).

Prominent Issue Areas Include Intellectual Property Rights for JCCT Commitments and Investment for S&ED Trade and Investment Commitments

We identified 184 commitments in the JCCT since 2004 and 114 trade and investment commitments in the S&ED since 2007 that involve China or China and the United States.[9] The commitments include statements affirming open trade principles, statements of policy intent, and statements that focus on trade actions specific to a sector. U.S. officials stressed that not all commitments are of equal value and significance.[10]

We examined the JCCT and S&ED commitments to provide an overview of their areas of emphasis and other characteristics. We identified 11 issue areas to characterize the content of each commitment, including sector-specific issues. Fifty-four percent of the JCCT commitments and 48 percent of the S&ED trade and investment commitments were related to two or three issue areas. See figure 2 for the list of issue areas and number of commitments related to each issue area. Table 2 in appendix I describes each issue area and provides examples of commitments.

At the JCCT, a large share of commitments are related to intellectual property rights (62 commitments or 34 percent)[11] and technical and regulatory barriers to trade (45 commitments or 24 percent). China has made commitments related to both of these issue areas every year since 2004, with at least 20 percent of commitments related to intellectual property rights and at least 10 percent of commitments related to technical and regulatory barriers to trade. In addition, 110 commitments (or 60 percent of all China's JCCT commitments) refer to a specific sector, including 28 commitments related to pharmaceuticals and medical devices, 19 commitments related to agriculture, and 18 commitments related to software use.[12]

For the S&ED, 70 percent of the trade and investment commitments are related to one or more of the following three issue areas: investment (30 commitments or 26 percent), multilateral issues (26 commitments or 23 percent), and transparency (24 commitments or 21 percent).

Differences in the number of commitments associated with specific issue areas across the two dialogues may reflect differences in the dialogues' structure and focus. According to U.S. officials, the JCCT has had greater focus on bilateral trade issues and sectors, in contrast with the S&ED, where trade and investment issues have been discussed within a broader range of economic and strategic issues. In addition, our analysis shows that statements of joint actions by China and the United States are more common at the S&ED

(75 percent). According to Treasury officials, this reflects the broad economic focus and cross-cutting discussions of the S&ED's economic track. The majority of China's JCCT commitments (76 percent) involve China alone.

Expected Timeframes of Commitment Implementation

Commitments in the two dialogues generally do not specify timeframes although according to U.S. officials, many commitments are either expected to be implemented by the next annual meeting or are considered to be ongoing. According to Commerce officials, that would be the case, for example, for a commitment by China to provide fair treatment to foreign investors.[13] According to Treasury officials, in the S&ED the two sides work under the general assumption, unless stated otherwise, that each year's S&ED commitments are to be implemented by the next S&ED meeting.[14] Some JCCT and S&ED commitments do specify a timeframe. Of the commitments we identified, timeframes were specified in 17 percent of China's 184 JCCT commitments and 18 percent of China's 114 S&ED trade and investment commitments. For example, at the 2011 JCCT meeting, China agreed to publish procedures for telecommunications network access license and radio type approval by the end of 2011. At the 2013 S&ED meeting, China committed to submit a new revised offer to join the WTO's Government Procurement Agreement (GPA) by the end of 2013.[15]

Some Commitments Have Been Reaffirmed and Others Have Evolved

Our analysis shows continuity of issues and objectives pursued at the two dialogues from 2004 through 2013. Some specific commitments have been made repeatedly, while others have evolved.

Within S&ED issue areas, some commitments have been reaffirmed over time. For example, in investment—which is associated with 26 percent of China's S&ED trade and investment commitments—the United States and China committed to bilateral investment treaty negotiations each year, with commitments becoming increasingly specific. The 2013 commitment stated that the bilateral investment treaty will provide national treatment at all phases of investment, including market access ("pre-establishment"), and be negotiated under a "negative list" approach."[16] In another example, China repeatedly affirmed its intent to follow the generally accepted principles and practices of sovereign wealth funds.

Other commitments illustrate how efforts to address trade barriers in an issue area or sector have evolved over time. For example, the United States has secured multiple commitments in both the JCCT and S&ED concerning the terms under which China will accede to the GPA. These have become increasingly specific, moving from initially seeking China's commitment to submit a revised accession offer to subsequently seeking commitments related to the specific elements of such an offer. USTR reported U.S. concerns with each offer in its annual *National Trade Estimate Reports on Foreign Trade Barriers* (NTE) for 2011 through 2013:

- At the May 2010 S&ED, China committed to submit a revised offer to accede to the GPA by July of that year, which it did. However, USTR reported that China could improve its next offer by, among other things, including sub-central entities and certain state-owned enterprises.
- At the December 2010 JCCT, China committed to submit a second revised offer—whose content would be based on intra-governmental consultations on the entities to be subject to the agreement—to join the GPA before the WTO Committee on Government Procurement's final meeting in 2011. USTR reported that China submitted the offer but that it excluded too many state-owned enterprises.
- At the May 2012 S&ED, China committed to submit a new comprehensive revised offer that responded to the requests of the GPA parties to the WTO Committee on Government Procurement before the committee's final meeting in 2012. China submitted its third revised offer in November 2012.

China's commitments in software have also evolved over time. We identified 22 software-related commitments—18 in the JCCT beginning in 2004 and 4 in the S&ED beginning in 2011. In 2004, China committed to extend an existing ban on the use of pirated software in central and local governments. This commitment continued in subsequent years with the inclusion of state-owned enterprises in 2006. In 2010, China committed to establish software asset management systems for government agencies and to allocate budgetary funds for purchasing, upgrading, and replacing agency software, and in 2012, China confirmed that it required state-owned enterprises to use legitimate software. In the S&ED, China committed to strengthening inspections to ensure legitimate government software use in 2011 and to extending software management pilot projects to the enterprise sector in 2012.

AGENCIES USE VARIOUS MEANS TO TRACK IMPLEMENTATION

U.S. agencies track the implementation of commitments through various means including interactions with their Chinese counterparts and outreach to industry. U.S. agencies identified JCCT working groups and mid-year reviews, discussions with Chinese officials while developing joint fact sheets prior to S&ED meetings, U.S. industry associations and companies, and U.S. officials based in China as key sources for information on progress. U.S. agencies use several tracking documents that capture information on the status of some commitments over time and do not have a single document that encompasses either dialogue. In addition, U.S. agencies have sought to identify commercial metrics such as increased sales to use as indicators of implementation progress where possible, but cited challenges in identifying appropriate data.

U.S. Agencies Track Information on Implementation through Several Means

U.S. agencies collect information on the status of commitment implementation through several means, including ongoing engagement with their Chinese counterparts in preparation for meetings, and regular outreach to domestic stakeholders. One important source of tracking information is the 16 JCCT working groups. The working groups each comprise U.S. and Chinese officials; some focus on specific industries, such as steel, and some on trade issues such as intellectual property. According to U.S. agency officials and documents, the JCCT has added working groups in response to changes in the trade relationship—for example, adding the Trade and Investment Working Group which covers a range of trade and investment issues.[17] U.S. agencies obtain updated information on implementation status from their Chinese counterparts at working group meetings. For example, Commerce and USTR officials received information from working group meetings about Chinese actions taken to shut down websites selling counterfeit medicines, in response to 2010 and 2011 JCCT commitments. Intellectual Property Rights working group officials stated that their working group has been instrumental in following the implementation of commitments to reduce end-user piracy of software by government agencies and state-owned enterprises.

The Office of Science and Technology Policy (OSTP) tracks implementation of commitments China makes at the Innovation Dialogue which are part of the overall S&ED commitments. Established in 2010 at the request of the U.S. and Chinese leaders of the S&ED, the Innovation Dialogue is a forum to share best practices in promoting innovation.[18] The dialogue established a working group of U.S. and Chinese private sector experts and government officials, which monitors implementation of commitments and advises on barriers to successful implementation.[19]

U.S. government officials also analyze commitment implementation while preparing the joint fact sheet for the coming year's S&ED plenary meeting, according to Treasury officials. Treasury solicits and compiles input from key U.S. federal agencies on their priorities, which it exchanges with its Chinese counterparts. They then negotiate the wording of the joint fact sheet. This process can identify information on the status of past commitments, as well as in some cases on follow-on commitments. USTR and Treasury officials stated that participants actively negotiate JCCT commitment language immediately before and during the JCCT plenary meetings, and Treasury officials said that joint fact sheet language is also actively discussed during the time of the S&ED plenary meetings.

In addition, in 2010, the United States and China instituted a mid-year review within the JCCT as an additional tool to track commitment implementation and to prepare for annual plenary meetings. According to a USTR official and our review of mid-year review agendas, the review focuses on selected priority commitments from the previous year and proposing outcomes for the upcoming plenary.

U.S. officials observed that discussions of the status of particular commitments take place across a wide range of settings aside from those directly related to the JCCT and S&ED. Treasury officials stated that they follow up on the implementation of certain types of S&ED commitments in various meetings with their Chinese counterparts, citing government procurement issues as particularly relevant for discussions with their counterparts at the Ministry of Finance, which leads on the issue. One agency cited mechanisms for engaging their Chinese counterparts, such as memoranda of understanding with provisions related to implementation of JCCT commitments. U.S. reports cited forums such as WTO standing committees and the APEC forum as examples of meetings where JCCT and S&ED trade and investment commitment implementation may be discussed. For example, according to WTO documents, China reported to the WTO Committee on Government Procurement that it expected to submit a revised offer on government procurement to the committee before the end of 2013, consistent with its 2013 S&ED commitment.

U.S. agencies obtain information on implementation status from U.S. industry and U.S. officials abroad. U.S. officials based in Washington told us they work with U.S. industry associations and companies in developing information on an ongoing basis on China's implementation progress. For example, USTR solicits written submissions from interested parties through the issuance of *Federal Register* notices issued in conjunction with the preparation of annual mandated reports. U.S. officials based in China provide information on implementation status in reporting to headquarters while preparing annual mandated reports on trade issues, such as the Special 301 Report (on intellectual property rights protection) and the NTE. Embassy staff submits cables on key issues that include discussions of the status of trade barriers raised in the JCCT. U.S. officials serving in China obtain feedback from industry representatives based in that country. For example, locally based industry representatives provided information to U.S. embassy officials that China had effectively implemented a 2009 JCCT commitment to eliminate redundant medical device product recall regulations. According to Treasury officials, they regularly solicit government and industry sources for information on S&ED priorities in preparation of and after each dialogue.

Various Documents Track Separate Aspects of Implementation Status

U.S. agency officials stated that they use various documents to track the status of implementation over time and that there is no single, consolidated document or system that captures the status of implementation of JCCT or S&ED commitments. USTR officials said that the preparation of documents used to brief senior officials in advance of formal meetings—such as annual plenary meetings, mid-term reviews, and ad hoc high level meetings between U.S. and Chinese officials—is one of the processes used for tracking the status of implementation. According to representatives of the JCCT's Intellectual

Property Rights working group, briefing papers, together with other sources, also serve as a useful record of the status of implementation, and can help to facilitate knowledge transfer in the event of personnel turnover.

According to Commerce officials, a Commerce staff person, designated to help coordinate Commerce's JCCT activities, maintained a spreadsheet for the official's own use in tracking follow-up on China's JCCT commitments. The official used the spreadsheet to identify actions taken on the commitments made in the current year and to facilitate briefing senior officials in advance of meetings. Commerce officials stated that this spreadsheet is not an interagency document and does not constitute a department or interagency position on the status of implementation of commitments.[20]

Agencies Generally Have Not Used Commercial Metrics to Track Implementation of Commitments

Some policymakers and private sector representatives have asked the administration to use commercial metrics (e.g., exports and sales) to track commitment implementation where possible. According to a senior agency official, framing commitments in terms of commercial results such as increased sales can focus attention on the ultimate goal of increased exports rather than on individual trade barriers, which may be removed but replaced by different trade barriers.

Although agency officials identified one JCCT or S&ED commitment directly linking a commercial metric (increased sales) to implementation, they cited the difficulty in identifying appropriate commercial metrics generally. In a 2012 S&ED commitment concerning intellectual property- intensive industries, the United States and China committed to create environments for their respective markets in which the level of sales of legitimate intellectual property-intensive products and services would increase in line with the two countries' status as globally significant producers and consumers.[21] In addition, officials indicated that it is easier to measure implementation of commitments that entail concrete and transparent legal actions – such as enactment of a law or other measure, or accession to a treaty – than to measure implementation of commitments to reaffirm existing policies or to a general policy direction.

LACK OF COMPREHENSIVE INFORMATION ON IMPLEMENTATION OF COMMITMENTS ACROSS REPORTS LIMITS UNDERSTANDING OF PROGRESS

USTR includes information in nine reports on trade barriers generally and efforts to address them, but does not provide comprehensive information to Congress and the public on the status of implementation of JCCT and S&ED trade and investment commitments. The reports focus on various aspects of trade barriers and market access and have different areas of focus and structures. Our analysis of selected commitments indicated that reporting on implementation status is not comprehensive because the reports are sometimes not clear and complete. This lack of comprehensive information makes it more difficult for policymakers to understand the progress made by the implementation of these commitments in removing trade barriers.

USTR Describes JCCT and S&ED Commitment Implementation Status in Several Trade-Related Reports

USTR reports on the status of trade barriers and market access broadly through nine reports, which it identified as the source for public information on JCCT and S&ED commitment implementation.[22] In its strategic plan for fiscal years 2013 through 2016, USTR identifies these reports as important for building congressional support for the administration's trade agenda by helping Congress gain a comprehensive understanding of the efforts the administration undertakes to dismantle trade barriers.[23] Further, it characterized the reports as important to the agency's commitment to transparency and accountability to Congress and stakeholders. In addition, the administration has identified the work of these bilateral dialogues in removing trade barriers in China as critical to the success of the national goal of doubling exports by the end of 2014.

The nine reports respond to statutory requirements and have different focuses and structures.[24] The China WTO Compliance report, the only one focusing solely on China trade issues, examines the status of commitments made by China in connection with its accession to the WTO. Since 2008, the China WTO Compliance report has included a section on bilateral engagement that describes the outcomes for the present year; information on the status of past commitments is not included in that section but can be found in other sections of the report. Others among the nine reports have a worldwide scope and may include information on a specific sector, trade barrier, or policy area, including information on China and on the JCCT and S&ED commitments where appropriate. *Section 1377 Review of Telecommunications Agreements*, for example, focuses on trade barriers in a specific sector and the NTE identifies key barriers to U.S. trade and describes barriers in a number of countries. Table 1 provides an overview of the nine reports.

Table 1. Key Annual Reports Addressing Trade Barriers with China

Report	Subject	Structure	Year first issued
Report to Congress on China's WTO Compliance	Reports annually on China's progress in complying with commitments made in connection with its accession to the WTO. The report also describes U.S. efforts to reduce trade barriers with China through bilateral and multilateral forums, U.S. enforcement actions, and priority issues.	Divides China's WTO commitments into 9 broad categories, including trading rights, services, and agriculture.[a] The only one of the nine reports that focuses on China.	2002
National Trade Estimate Report on Foreign Trade Barriers	Identifies the most important foreign barriers to U.S. trade and provides some information on some of the actions taken to eliminate them.	Is organized by country and by nine categories including import policies, government procurement, intellectual property rights, and investment barriers.[b]	1985
Special 301 Report	Identifies trade barriers related to intellectual property rights and categorizes countries according to three levels of concern, with Priority Foreign Country designating the	Provides overview of global intellectual property issues and trends and also country-specific trends.[d] According to USTR, elements of an action plan are included in the	1989

Table 1. (Continued)

Report	Subject	Structure	Year first issued
	highest level.[c] China has been on the Priority Watch List since 2005.	Intellectual Property Rights working group discussions of the JCCT.[e]	
Section 1377 Review of Telecommunications Agreements	Indentifies trade barriers related to compliance with trade agreements relevant to the telecommunications sector (e.g., General Agreement on Tariffs and Trade).	Has focused on issues such as limits on foreign investment, competition. Not organized by country.	1989
Report on Technical Barriers to Trade	Identifies standards-related barriers to U.S. exports; provides a focal point for U.S. efforts to resolve standards-related barriers; and documents actions underway.[f]	Includes general information on standards-related measures and chapters on each of 17 countries, plus the European Union. Identifies the JCCT as a key bilateral forum to resolve standards-related issues.	2010
Report on Sanitary and Phytosanitary Measures	Identifies sanitary and phytosanitary barriers to U.S. exports; provides a focal point for U.S. efforts to resolve standards-related barriers; documents the actions underway.[g]	Describes unwarranted measures and explains why they impose barriers to trade, and how the United States is seeking to address them.	2010
Subsidies Enforcement Annual Report to the Congress	Describes the activities of the U.S. subsidies enforcement program.	Describes multilateral subsidy negotiations and ongoing enforcement and monitoring; report includes a section on China's WTO subsidy notification obligations.	1996

Report	Subject	Structure	Year first issued
Trade Policy Agenda and Annual Report of the President of the United States on the Trade Agreements Program	Provides an update on the trade agreements program and articulates the national trade policy agenda for that year.[h]	Describes the President's trade agenda for coming year and reports on last year's activities. Includes discussions for specific regions and countries.	1957
Report by the Office of the United States Trade Representative on Trade-Related Barriers to the Export of Greenhouse Gas Intensity Reducing Technologies	Provides an update on the progress made in removing the trade barriers that U.S. exporters of green technologies face in the top 25 greenhouse gas emitting developing countries. The report also aims to describe U.S. efforts to reduce these barriers.	Since 2008, report has appeared as an appendix to the NTE report. For specific trade barriers in top emitting developing countries— which include China— see relevant sections of the NTE and Special 301 reports.	2006

Source: cited reports, the Office of the U.S. Trade Representative.

Notes:

[a] These categories are (1) trading rights, (2) services, (3) import regulation, (4) export regulation, (5) internal policies affecting trade, (6) investment, (7) agriculture, (8) intellectual property rights, (and (9) legal framework.

[b] The nine categories are: (1) import policies, (2) government procurement, (3) export subsidies, (4) lack of intellectual property protection, (5) service barriers, (6) investment barriers, (7) government- tolerated anti-competitive conduct, (8) trade restrictions affecting electronic commerce, and (9) other barriers. Other barriers are those that encompass more than one category (e.g., transparency) or affect a single sector).

[c] USTR indicates concern with a trade barrier related to intellectual property rights by placing countries on a "Priority Watch List" or "Watch List." The United States focuses its bilateral diplomatic efforts to improve intellectual property rights protection on Priority Watch List designees. Those countries that have the most egregious policies, acts, or practices with respect to intellectual property rights protection are designated as "Priority Foreign Countries."

[d] USTR stated that the China section of the Special 301 report is the most comprehensive in the report and provides a means to track progress on issues.

[e] The United States develops action plans and similar programs to address intellectual property rights issues in various contexts, including the Special 301 process.

According to USTR, these plans and programs establish benchmarks, such as legislative, policy, or regulatory action by which to measure progress in improving intellectual property rights protection. In May 2011, USTR invited any country appearing on the Special 301 Priority Watch List or Watch List to negotiate a mutually agreed action plan designed to lead to that country's removal from the relevant list.

[f] According to the introduction to the report, standards-related measures are documents and procedures that set out specific technical or other requirements for products or processes as well as procedures to ensure that these requirements are met.

[g] Sanitary and phytosanitary measures, which are measures that governments apply to protect human, animal, or plant life or health from risks arising from the entry or spread of plant- or animal- borne pests or diseases, or from additives, contaminants, toxins, or disease-causing organisms in foods, beverages, or feedstuffs.

[h] According to the International Trade Commission, "the trade agreements program includes 'all activities consisting of, or related to, the administration of international agreements which primarily concern trade and which are concluded pursuant to the authority vested in the President by the Constitution' and congressional legislation."

USTR officials told us that the WTO Compliance report is the primary report on the status of the implementation of commitments, and the other eight reports contain additional information on some commitments. USTR prepares these nine reports with assistance from Commerce, Treasury, and other agencies on the Trade Policy Staff Committee.[25] Such assistance includes reporting from U.S. embassies, reviewing drafts to ensure accuracy and, in the case of the China WTO Compliance and Special 301 reports, holding public hearings to obtain private sector views. For instance, a senior Treasury official told us that Treasury participates in the preparation of the China WTO Compliance report by reviewing a draft for accuracy.

In addition to this public reporting, Commerce, USTR, and Treasury officials stated that they inform stakeholders on the status of implementation through briefings to industry associations and to members of Congress and their staffs, participation in congressional hearings, and briefings to the trade advisory committees. Further, agency officials said they have briefed Congress repeatedly on broader U.S. engagement with China. Agency officials told us that while they did not generally provide reports to accompany the briefings, they may bring fact sheets, remarks, and recent speeches; we did not identify additional regular documentary reporting on the status of implementation of JCCT and S&ED commitments beyond the public reports.

Reports Lack Clear and Comprehensive Information on Status of Implementation of JCCT and S&ED Trade and Investment Commitments

Our review of reporting on implementation status revealed challenges to obtaining clear and comprehensive information. For some commitments, the reports lack information on the status of implementation and for some the reporting is not clear.[26] Additionally, differences in the formats of the reports make locating information on a given commitment or issue area across reports difficult in some cases. The lack of detailed information on China's progress in implementing certain commitments makes it difficult for Congress and other stakeholders to fully understand the progress the United States is making in reducing trade barriers.

Our analysis found several instances of incomplete reporting on the status of specific commitments related to market access barriers in sectors, such as software, and in cross-cutting areas such as industrial policy.[27] For example,

- We identified 9 commitments from the 2008-2011 JCCT, and 1 from the 2011 S&ED related to software legalization.[28] Based on our analysis of the nine reports identified above, we were not able to clearly identify the implementation status of most of these specific commitments. For example, USTR has not reported on whether China has increased resources devoted to conducting audits and inspections as it committed to do at the 2011 JCCT.
- A second software legalization example illustrates a lack of clarity across reports on implementation status. At the 2011 JCCT, China committed to complete software legalization programs at the provincial level by the middle of 2012 and to publish the results of its software audits. The 2013 NTE report indicated that, because of a lack of published information, USTR could not verify that China had completed a program to ensure provincial governments used legal software. However, the 2013 Special 301 report, issued a month later, stated that China had completed the program. In addition to the difference regarding completion status of the legalization program at the provincial level, it is unclear whether China has implemented its related commitment to publish the results of audits. Thus, it cannot be determined whether the gap in implementation is one of program completion or one of reporting.

- There has not been reporting on implementation of commitments concerning certain Chinese industrial policies. Specifically, at the 2011 JCCT, China committed to ensure open and transparent processes for developing standards for smart-grid products and technologies. USTR has not reported on the status of implementation of this commitment, despite having a specific report that describes progress in greenhouse gas reducing technologies. The greenhouse gas reports issued in 2012 and 2013 do not describe the steps taken in the JCCT regarding this issue.
- USTR has not reported on the implementation of some commitments made by China related to its use of technical standards to favor domestic suppliers. In the 2011 JCCT, China reported on the development and publication of revised safety standards for medical devices, acknowledged the value of closer cooperation with the United States on those standards, and committed to participate in an information exchange program with the United States in 2012. The status of that commitment was not addressed in either the 2012 or 2013 reports.
- Reporting on implementation of China's commitments to reform state-owned enterprises has been incomplete. In the 2010 S&ED, China committed to continue its reform of these entities by, among other actions, inviting non-public and foreign investors to take equity stakes in them. China also committed at the 2010 JCCT that all enterprises in China, including state-owned enterprises, will make purchases and sales based solely on commercial considerations. As part of that same commitment, it committed to leave such decisions to those entities and to provide equal treatment to public and private enterprises. USTR has not reported on the status of implementation of these commitments in any of the nine trade-related reports.

In addition to incomplete or unclear reporting on the status of implementation of some commitments, differing report structures make it difficult in some cases to obtain information across reports. For example, we found reporting relevant to a 2010 S&ED commitment on new energy technologies discussed in the import barriers section of the NTE report's chapter on China, whereas the WTO Compliance report discussed it under investment. Similarly, with respect to a 2012 JCCT commitment by China to issue a catalogue for the purchase of official use vehicles, the WTO Compliance report discussed the commitment in the intellectual property rights section, and the NTE report discussed it in a newly created category for the China chapter of the report, "Indigenous Innovation, Technology Transfer and Strategic Emerging Industry Barriers."

In interviews and documents, agency officials emphasized the need to balance reporting on the status of implementation of commitments with the requirement to avoid disclosures that would disadvantage the United States in ongoing consultations. For example, in the NTE report, USTR indicates that it does not provide estimates of the impact of trade barriers that are the subject of ongoing consultations to avoid disrupting them. In the case of the trade agenda, USTR may submit classified information to Congress in confidence, if it deems necessary.

The absence of clear and complete reporting on the status of implementation of commitments makes it difficult for policymakers to gain a comprehensive understanding of the progress made toward reducing trade barriers through the implementation of commitments from the dialogues. Moreover, accountability is reinforced through public reporting of agency results and, if appropriate, confidential reporting to Congress.

CONCLUSION

China has made a significant number and wide array of commitments to the United States in the JCCT and S&ED, high-level bilateral U.S.-China dialogues which address trade issues. While information on the commitments is available from agency fact sheets, information on the status of implementation is not presented in a manner that provides a comprehensive understanding of China's overall progress in implementing the commitments. Although at least nine reports present information on the status of U.S. efforts to decrease trade barriers with China, in some cases referencing the JCCT and S&ED, obtaining specific information on implementation status from the reports presents challenges. These nine reports aim to provide a comprehensive picture of the administration's efforts to address trade barriers through consultative mechanisms such as the JCCT and S&ED. Without comprehensive reporting—easily accessible in one location and complete—it is difficult for external parties to understand the progress being made in removing barriers to this very important export market through bilateral dialogue. More consolidated and complete information on the status of China's implementation of its JCCT commitments and S&ED trade and investment commitments would give policymakers a better basis to identify areas of success or failure.

RECOMMENDATION FOR EXECUTIVE ACTION

To improve policymakers' and the public's understanding of progress through bilateral dialogues in increasing access to China's markets, we recommend that the U.S. Trade Representative, in conjunction with the Secretary of Commerce and the Secretary of the Treasury, work to provide clearer and more comprehensive reporting on the status of China's implementation of its JCCT and S&ED trade and investment commitments. This reporting should include more complete information on the status of implementation of these commitments, as well as a more clearly identified source for consolidated information, which could be an existing report.

AGENCY COMMENTS AND OUR EVALUATION

We provided a draft of this report to Commerce, USTR, Treasury, State, USDA, and OSTP. Commerce and USTR provided written comments. Commerce, USTR, Treasury, USDA, and OSTP provided technical comments which we incorporated as appropriate.

Neither Commerce nor USTR directly agreed or disagreed with our recommendation. Commerce stated that it would take GAO's ideas and findings under careful consideration, but expressed concern regarding our conclusion that lack of comprehensive reporting makes it difficult for external parties to understand progress made in bilateral trade dialogues with China. It further observed that assessments of reporting needs should include consideration of resource requirements. We agree that resource considerations are a key factor in agency approaches to reporting, but believe that steps to make information on commitment implementation status more comprehensive and accessible can be taken.

USTR stated that it welcomed GAO's suggestions and would consider them carefully, but identified several concerns. First, USTR expressed its view that some commitments are more noteworthy than others and counting and categorizing commitments can be misleading when used as the basis for conclusions about the relative significance of issue areas. We agree that not all commitments are of equal significance and reflected that view in our draft report. We believe, however, that summary quantitative information is one useful tool for conveying information about the issues addressed in these dialogues.

USTR commented that the report's discussion of agencies' tracking of the implementation of China's commitments is generally accurate, but stated that the role of U.S. stakeholders such as industry associations and companies is not adequately reflected in the report. We agree that such organizations are an important source of information on commitment implementation and have added additional information in the report to reflect their role.

With respect to U.S. agency reporting on commitment implementation, USTR stated that in its view the Administration's written reporting currently provides congressional policymakers and other stakeholders comprehensive information on China's implementation of JCCT and S&ED commitments, and stated that it also meets with those parties on these issues. It stated that not all JCCT and S&ED commitments warrant discussion in the reports, but acknowledged that GAO's analysis identifies commitments whose implementation status should be reported on and has not been. Based on extensive analysis of agency reporting on the implementation of these commitments, we concluded that information on the status of commitments made in these bilateral dialogues with China is not complete and easily accessible, which can make it difficult for policymakers to identify areas of success and failure and assess options for moving forward. We recognize that meetings with policymakers and stakeholders are also an important part agency communication on these issues.

David Gootnick
Director, International Affairs and Trade

APPENDIX I. OBJECTIVES, SCOPE, AND METHODOLOGY

In this report, we (1) describe the commitments China made at the Joint Commission on Commerce and Trade (JCCT) and the trade and investment commitments China made at the Strategic and Economic Dialogue (S&ED),[29] (2) describe U.S. agency tracking of China's implementation of these commitments, and (3) evaluate U.S. agency reporting on the status of commitment implementation.

To conduct this review, we interviewed knowledgeable U.S. government officials from the Department of Commerce (Commerce), the Office of the U.S. Trade Representative (USTR), the Departments of the Treasury (Treasury), State (State), and Agriculture (USDA) as well as the Office of Science and Technology Policy (OSTP) in Washington, D.C., and in Beijing, China (via a videoconference). We also interviewed representatives of trade associations and research organizations.

To describe the commitments, we conducted a detailed review of the fact sheets issued at the conclusion of annual meetings at the JCCT from 2004 through 2012, the S&ED from 2009 through 2013, and the SED from 2006 through 2008. Commerce and USTR issue a JCCT fact sheet; Treasury issues jointly with China an S&ED fact sheet for the economic track that presents the joint commitments negotiated by the United States and China. (Treasury also issues a U.S. fact sheet that discusses the benefits of the commitments for U.S. workers and companies.) According to senior Commerce, USTR, and Treasury officials, the fact sheets present the commitments negotiated between the U.S. and Chinese governments. In addition to presenting the commitments, the fact sheets also contain details of cooperative activities between the two countries. We used the joint fact sheets for our analysis of China's S&ED commitments because, according to senior officials, they reflect the two governments' understanding of the results of the S&ED plenary meeting. For the S&ED, we limited our analysis to China's commitments in the trade and investment pillar of the dialogue's economic track.[30] In our analysis, "S&ED commitments" refer to the trade and investment commitments China made in the S&ED in 2009 through 2013 and in the SED in 2007 and 2008.

We discussed the fact sheets with cognizant officials from Commerce and USTR, the two agencies that jointly lead the JCCT for the United States, and from Treasury, which leads the S&ED's economic track for the United States, to obtain an understanding of the information they contain and how they are put together. According to senior USTR officials, the commitments as presented in the fact sheets are high-level political commitments and are the outcomes of the structured dialogues established to address and resolve a range of issues. While the outcomes documents are not legal instruments, the commitments are taken seriously, according to these officials.

To identify the commitments, we separated the fact sheet text describing steps taken by China into individual commitments, created a database, and systematically analyzed individual commitments. The fact sheets state China's commitments, U.S. commitments, and joint U.S-China commitments. We excluded fact sheet text reflecting U.S. commitments, but included statements about commitments made jointly by the United States and China and by China alone.

We identified 184 JCCT commitments and 114 S&ED trade and investment commitments. (An inventory of the commitments we identified and their categorization by issue area, described below, is provided in an online e-supplement, GAO-14-224SP.) JCCT fact sheets, written by the U.S. government, are typically written in bulleted form, with each bullet generally considered by us as one commitment. S&ED fact sheets are different in that the precise wording of every commitment is negotiated jointly by the U.S. and Chinese governments. The 2013 S&ED fact sheet listed the trade and investment commitments in bulleted format. Prior to that, the commitments were written in paragraphs that included statements on multiple topics. The JCCT and S&ED fact sheets vary in terms of the number of areas and activities addressed, and in the specificity of the statements. We discussed with U.S. agencies ways to identify and count specific commitments in fact sheets, and determined that there is no single way to do so. For example, an analysis of the S&ED fact sheets for 2009 through 2012 might treat a paragraph as a commitment. We chose to break some paragraphs into multiple commitments, using decision rules that we developed to ensure the consistency and completeness of this exercise. These included whether the paragraph referred to more than one intended action or discrete concept, and whether it specified a deadline. In addition, if the same or similarly worded commitment was made in multiple years, we counted it anew each time.

After identifying individual commitments, we categorized them by several characteristics (issue areas, joint or China-only, deadline). We identified 11 issue areas to characterize the content of each commitment after an iterative review of all of the commitments in our database by several analysts. To support development of these categories we used as a reference point categories developed in a previous GAO report on China's commitments[31] as well as the headers used in JCCT source documents. (S&ED fact sheets do not use headers and sub-headers for the commitments in the trade and investment pillar.) These were adapted and recombined producing a set of categories that took into account the specific language of the specific sets of commitments from recent years and covered both dialogues. See the list of issue areas with descriptions and examples in table 2.

We then assessed each commitment for the issue area(s) it covered. Because many commitments covered multiple issue areas, we assigned up to three issue areas to each commitment. Ninety-nine of the 184 JCCT commitments and 55 of the 114 S&ED commitments were associated with two or three issue areas. We identified some commitments that did not fit any of the 11 issue areas and categorized these commitments as "other."

Table 2. List of Issue Areas Identified in GAO's Analysis of China's JCCT Commitments (2004-2012) and S&ED Trade and Investment Commitments (2007-2013)

	Issue area	Description of issue area	Examples of commitments associated with issue area
1	Government procurement	Includes policies for purchase of goods and services by government and by state-owned enterprises as well as negotiations for China's accession to the World Trade Organization (WTO) Agreement on Government Procurement.[a]	The United States and China recognize the importance of non-discriminatory government procurement policies. To that end, the United States and China agree to strengthen their cooperation in order to accelerate China's accession to the WTO Government Procurement Agreement. This will include China's submission, to the WTO Government Procurement Committee before the Committee's October 2009 meeting, of a report that sets out the improvements that China will make in its revised offer. (S&ED, 2009)
2	High technology trade	Includes promotion of U.S. high technology exports to China.	Continue cooperation through the JCCT High Technology and Strategic Trade Working Group by positively implementing "Guidelines for U.S.-China High Technology and Strategic Trade Development" and taking appropriate constructive measures and working out an action plan to expand and facilitate bilateral high-tech and strategic trade. (SED, 2007)

	Issue area	Description of issue area	Examples of commitments associated with issue area
3	Innovation	Includes measures promoting "indigenous innovation"[b] and linkages between innovation policies and government procurement preferences.	The relevant Chinese departments are conducting further modifications to the Implementing Regulations on the Government Procurement Law and will seriously take into account opinions and suggestions from all sides, including from the United States. In government procurement, China will give equal treatment to all innovation products produced in China by foreign-invested enterprises and Chinese-invested enterprises alike. (The United States expressed concerns that under Article 9 of China's draft Regulations, product lists could be used to provide government procurement preferences to indigenous innovation products.) (JCCT, 2010)
4	Intellectual property rights	Includes laws and regulations providing for the protection and enforcement of intellectual property rights, such as copyrights, trademarks, and patents.	China and the United States agreed to continue cooperation on strengthening library intellectual property rights protection and to continue exchanging views and sharing information with rights holders about library intellectual property rights protection efforts. Specifically, China's National Copyright Administration described its ongoing efforts to investigate complaints by academic journal publishers about web-based enterprises piracy of library academic journals, and agreed to take

Table 2. (Continued)

	Issue area	Description of issue area	Examples of commitments associated with issue area
			prompt action at the conclusion of its investigations. (JCCT, 2010)
5	Investment	Includes laws, regulations, and other measures that limit foreign investment, such as regulations on mergers and acquisitions involving foreign investors.	China commits to provide fair treatment to foreign investors in China. China is to focus its security review over mergers and acquisitions by foreign capital solely on national security concerns and adhere to specific timelines and review standards. China is to continue to simplify its foreign investment approval system and enhance transparency on a step-by-step basis. During the 12th Five Year Plan period, China is to implement a more proactive opening-up strategy and expand the areas open to foreign investment and the degree of openness. (S&ED, 2012)
6	Multilateral issues	Includes references to international agreements and consistency of domestic laws, regulations, and practices with multilateral commitments.	China has committed to improve protection of electronic data by ratifying and implementing the World Intellectual Property Organization Internet Treaties as soon as possible [and] extending an existing ban on the use of pirated software in central government and provincial agencies to include local governments. (JCCT, 2004) The United States and China recognize that it is critical to follow WTO rules

	Issue area	Description of issue area	Examples of commitments associated with issue area
			when initiating trade remedy investigations and imposing trade remedy measures, to prevent their abuse, and commit to refrain from using such measures for purposes other than trade remedies themselves, including to achieve industrial policy objectives. The two sides commit to respect the decisions of the WTO dispute settlement mechanism. Both sides commit to handle anti-dumping and countervailing duty investigations in a fair, objective, and transparent manner. (S&ED, 2012)
7	Open trade principles	Includes statements affirming commitment to open trade and investment.	Against the background of deteriorating economic conditions worldwide, the U.S. and China highlighted the importance of and their shared commitment to fighting protectionism and promoting open trade and investment. (SED, 2008)
8	Sector-specific issues	Includes measures and policies— such as custom duties, tariff-rate quotas, export subsidies, domestic support, and restrictions on imports for health and environmental reasons— that limit market access for U.S. companies in specific sectors or industries.	Agriculture: China agreed to immediately allow seven U.S. poultry processing plants to resume exports to China. [The United States has] urged China to work to address underlying systemic issues to eliminate such problems in the future. (JCCT, 2008) Software: China is to further promote the use of legal software by state-owned enterprises, including by strengthening supervision of central state-owned

Table 2. (Continued)

	Issue area	Description of issue area	Examples of commitments associated with issue area
			enterprises and large state-owned financial institutions by establishing software asset management systems; enforcing China's requirement to purchase and use legitimate software by these state-owned enterprises; providing budget guarantees for software and promoting centralized procurement. The United States and China are to strengthen cooperation to address technical implementation issues, in order to consolidate the software legalization achievements. (S&ED, 2013)
9	Technical and regulatory barriers to trade	Includes non-tariff trade barriers in the form of product standards, technical requirements, testing, and certification, as well as regulatory barriers to trade.	Technical: China will consider an exemption of requiring product samples to be tested in Chinese test labs prior to approval if the manufacturer demonstrates compliance with international standards and provides sound scientific evidence. (JCCT, 2009) Regulatory: China agreed to convene another meeting of the U.S.-China Insurance Dialogue before the end of 2005 to discuss regulatory concerns and barriers to further liberalization of the sector. (JCCT, 2005)
10	Trade remedies	Includes subsidies providing economic benefit granted by a government to domestic producers of	China will provide a detailed accounting of its subsidies to the WTO by the end of 2005. (JCCT, 2005)

	Issue area	Description of issue area	Examples of commitments associated with issue area
		goods or services, often to strengthen their competetive position, as well as laws and regulations related to antidumping and countervailing duties.	Both sides decided to prioritize work during the next six months in several areas: Launch agreement consultations to facilitate Chinese group leisure travel to the United States, continue discussions on the possibility of a bilateral investment agreement, and strengthen consultation and cooperation on China's market economy status. (SED, 2007) Both sides agreed to continue consultation through the JCCT and other channels on trade remedy rules and procedure. (SED, 2008)
11	Transparency	Includes efforts to improve the openness of China's trade regime by, for example, publishing proposed regulations, providing clarifying information on rules, laws, or processes, or providing opportunities to comment on draft regulations.	China and the United States reaffirm their prior SED outcomes on transparency. The United States welcomes China's statement that it will issue a measure in 2011, to implement the requirement to publish all proposed trade- and economic-related administrative regulations and departmental rules on the State Council Legislative Affairs Office (SCLAO) website for a public comment period of not less than 30 days from the date of publication, except as specified in China's Protocol of Accession to the WTO or in public emergency situations. China will steadily increase its solicitation of public

Table 2. (Continued)

	Issue area	Description of issue area	Examples of commitments associated with issue area
			opinions on regulatory documents with a direct influence on the rights and obligations of citizens, legal persons, or other organizations. (S&ED, 2011)
12	Other	Includes statements of cooperation on such issues as rules of origin, counter-terrorism, sub-national cooperation, trade financing, market access for U.S. small- and medium-sized enterprises, Chinese value-added tax (VAT), and others.	Both sides agreed to strengthen cooperation on Rules of Origin, Customs Trade Partnership Against Terrorism, and the protection of cultural relics. (SED, 2008) China confirmed that a Ministry of Finance-led delegation would hold discussions with the United States, beginning in the first half of 2013, in order to work toward a mutual understanding of China's VAT system and the concepts on which a trade neutral VAT system is based. (JCCT, 2012)

Source: GAO analysis of JCCT and S&ED fact sheets; U.S. agency and WTO reports.

Notes:

[a] The WTO Government Procurement Agreement (GPA) is a plurilateral agreement that currently covers the United States and 41 other WTO members. China is not yet a party to the GPA. The GPA applies to the procurement of goods and services by central and sub-central government agencies and government enterprises specified by each party, subject to specified thresholds and certain exceptions. It requires GPA parties to provide most-favored-nation and national treatment to the goods, services and suppliers of other GPA parties and to conduct their procurement in accordance with procedures designed to ensure transparency, fairness and predictability in the procurement process. China has committed in its WTO accession agreement that all of its central and local government entities will conduct their procurements in a transparent manner until China completes its accession to the GPA.

b Indigenous innovation" policies promote the development, commercialization, and purchase of Chinese products and technologies and may disadvantage U.S. and other foreign firms and create new barriers to foreign direct investment and exports to China. These policies are often embedded in government procurement, technical standards, anti-monopoly policy, and tax laws and regulations. See U.S. International Trade Commission, *China: Intellectual Property Infringement, Indigenous Innovation Policies, and Frameworks for Measuring the Effects on the U.S. Economy*, Publication 4199, November 2010.

Many commitments, including 110 JCCT and 11 S&ED commitments, were related to specific sectors (see examples for agriculture and software in table 2). We identified 15 sectors: agriculture, distribution/retail, information technology and security, insurance, new energy vehicles, pharmaceuticals and medical devices, postal/courier, shipping, software, steel, telecommunications, textiles, transportation, travel and tourism, and wind power. We discussed this methodology with officials from Commerce, USTR, Treasury, State, and USDA.

To ensure the validity of this analysis we performed multiple sets of reviews and checks. Initial testing of subsets of the commitments was done by two analysts and a methodologist. The full analysis of all commitments was performed by two analysts who cross-checked each other's analysis and reconciled differences through discussion. A methodologist provided a spot-check of the analysis. Finally, the full team met and discussed in detail every commitment to ensure final consensus on the issue area categorization.

To describe how agencies track the status of implementation of commitments, we interviewed officials and reviewed documents from Commerce, USTR, Treasury, State, USDA, and OSTP. We also discussed these issues with U.S. embassy staff in Beijing, via videoconference. We discussed with the officials their processes for tracking commitment status, and sought corroborating information where needed. For example, we sought corroborating information from officials concerning their engagement with China in other various bilateral and multilateral forums, and their obtaining input from industry stakeholders and U.S. government officials based overseas. We corroborated this information by reviewing public reports from the outcomes of other diplomatic forums such as minutes from World Trade Organization standing committee meetings and public comments submitted by industry officials in conjunction with agency preparation of public reports.[32] We also reviewed a cable from the 2010 JCCT mid-year review and a cable about the 2010 S&ED annual meeting. Finally, we reviewed agendas for the

2010-2012 JCCT mid-term reviews. We also interviewed industry associations.

With respect to the use of tools such as tracking sheets to maintain and share information on commitment implementation, we discussed agency staff-level methods for tracking the status of commitments with officials from Commerce. For contextual purposes, we also discussed with State officials their process for tracking the status of commitments in the strategic track of the S&ED. We discussed with Commerce staff the characteristics and use of a tracking document developed by staff for compiling information on commitment implementation for use in briefing senior officials for key meetings.

To evaluate how U.S. agencies report on the status of commitment implementation, we asked agency officials and consulted agency documents to identify relevant public documents and other types of reports they use to inform the public and Congress on the outcomes and status. They identified nine reports that describe administration efforts to reduce trade barriers through negotiations, consultations and dispute settlement, which are identified in the body of this report. To make assessments of the reporting that we identified across the reporting documents, we focused primarily on identifying information that specifically referenced the status of implementation of the commitment by the Chinese government or other relevant Chinese entities. To assess the completeness of the reporting, we examined the nine reports for information on the status of implementation of commitments made in the JCCT and the S&ED in 2010 and 2011 and in additional years—2008 and 2009—related to software legalization. We examined these commitments related to software legalization because intellectual property was a prominent JCCT issue area and we had identified software earlier in our review as a potential illustrative area. For each of these commitments, we reviewed reporting subsequent to when the commitment was made. The assessment included keyword searches of the nine reports.. For example, for a software legalization commitment we performed keyword searches using "software," "legalization," and other terms specific to the commitment. We also did a more general reading of reporting language relevant to a given commitment. This analysis was reviewed by a second analyst and any differences the reviewer had with the original analysis were reconciled.

We reviewed the congressional budget justifications for Commerce, USTR, Treasury, and USDA to describe how U.S. efforts to track and report on the status of China's implementation of commitments supported agency and administration goals. We also reviewed comments from industry representatives submitted in conjunction with the preparation of statutory reports.

We conducted this performance audit from May 2012 to February 2014 in accordance with generally accepted government auditing standards. Those standards require that we plan and perform the audit to obtain sufficient, appropriate evidence to provide a reasonable basis for our findings and conclusions based on our audit objectives. We believe that the evidence obtained provides a reasonable basis for our findings and conclusions based on our audit objectives.

End Notes

[1] For simplicity of exposition, when we refer to "trade and investment commitments China made at the S&ED" we mean commitments made by China in the SED in 2007 and 2008 and in the S&ED from 2009 through 2013.

[2] According to senior officials from the Department of Commerce, Office of the U.S. Trade Representative, and the Department of the Treasury, the commitments presented in the fact sheets are the official commitments negotiated with the Chinese government.

[3] According to the Office of the U.S. Trade Representative, trade barriers, broadly defined, are government laws, regulations, policies, or practices that either protect domestic goods and services from foreign competition, artificially stimulate exports of particular domestic goods and services, or fail to provide adequate and effective protection of intellectual property rights.

[4] APEC is the primary economic forum in the Asia-Pacific region. Established in 1989 and comprising 21 member economies, including the United States, APEC aims to facilitate economic cooperation and to expand trade and investment throughout the region. WTO standing committees are issue-based groups that meet regularly to permit WTO members to exchange views, work to resolve questions of members' compliance with commitments, and develop initiatives aimed at systemic improvements.

[5] The JCCT was co-chaired by the U.S. Secretary of Commerce and China's Minister of Commerce from 1983 through 2003, when the two sides agreed to elevate the dialogue's leadership in order to address high priority trade issues more effectively.

[6] The other three pillars of the S&ED's economic track focus on macroeconomic cooperation, global economic governance, and financial markets. The United States and China discuss financial services trade issues under the financial markets pillar.

[7] Some commitments that are not presented in the fact sheets as "cooperative activities" also focus on cooperation. For example, a commitment in the 2010 JCCT fact sheet states that China and the United States agreed to work closely to cooperate and conduct information exchange concerning counterfeit drug activities and agreed to provide information about cases of counterfeit drugs through regulatory channels.

[8] The "S&ED commitments" in our analysis refer to trade and investment commitments China made at the S&ED and its predecessor, SED. They do not include S&ED strategic track commitments or economic commitments outside of the trade and investment pillar.

[9] We excluded commitments that involved only the United States.

[10] Our analysis does not address the relative significance of the commitments.

[11] As defined in the WTO's Agreement on Trade-Related Aspects of Intellectual Property Rights, intellectual property rights include copyright and related rights as well as protection of trademarks, geographical indications, industrial designs, patents, integrated circuit layout-designs, and undisclosed information, including trade secrets.

[12] If the same commitment was made repeatedly in different years, we counted it as a separate commitment in each year.

[13] Commerce officials further noted that U.S. understanding of when commitments are to be implemented is shaped by the larger context of those commitments. For example, these officials observed that China's legislative calendar has a bearing on the U.S. government's understanding of when China is to implement legislative changes discussed in JCCT commitments.

[14] The joint 2013 S&ED fact sheet explicitly stated that "[t]he two countries reached consensus to work expeditiously to implement the commitments made and, as the Special Representatives of the Economic Track, directed their respective economic teams to take concrete steps before the next Strategic and Economic Dialogue to do so."

[15] The GPA is a plurilateral agreement that currently covers the United States and 41 other WTO members. China is not yet a party to the GPA. The agreement requires GPA parties to provide most-favored-nation and national treatment to the goods, services and suppliers of other GPA parties and to conduct their procurement in accordance with procedures designed to ensure transparency, fairness and predictability in the procurement process. China has committed in its WTO accession agreement that all of its central and local government entities will conduct their procurements in a transparent manner until China completes its accession to the GPA.

[16] Pre-establishment refers to the entry of investments and investors of one member country of a trade or investment agreement into the territory of another. Each member country allows investors of other member countries to establish an investment in their territory on terms no less favorable than those that apply to domestic investors (national treatment) or investors from third countries (most-favored-nation treatment). Pre- establishment is rarely granted without exceptions since every country has sensitive sectors where foreign investment is not permitted. A negative list approach requires that discriminatory measures affecting all included sectors of a trade or investment agreement be liberalized unless specific measures are set out in the list of reservations.

[17] The groups are active to varying degrees; the Intellectual Property Rights working group meets twice a year while the Steel Dialogue has met four times since its creation in 2005.

[18] The Innovation Dialogue is led by the Director of the U.S. Office of Science and Technology Policy and China's Minister of Science and Technology.

[19] This dialogue has also resulted in negotiation of new commitments. In a commitment reported in the 2012 S&ED fact sheet, and negotiated in the Innovation Dialogue, China committed to treat intellectual property owned or developed in other countries in the same manner as intellectual property owned or developed in China. According to OSTP officials, following concerns raised by the private sector concerning tax preferences that appeared to favor Chinese firms, the Innovation Dialogue negotiated a new commitment by China to review these preferences.

[20] As an example of a different tracking approach, State Department officials stated that they do use a single spreadsheet to track the status of commitments made in the strategic track of the S&ED. They cited a document they maintain which has in the past been shared with officials at other agencies.

[21] In 2012, Commerce identified the industries that most intensively use patents and trademarks as well as those responsible for most of the creation and production of copyrighted materials. Commerce defined the 75 industries that were the most patent, trademark, and copyright intensive as "intellectual property-intensive."

[22] Specifically, USTR states that, collectively, the reports identify the major trade barriers to U.S. exports and the administration's efforts to dismantle them through negotiation, consultation, and dispute settlement. The JCCT and the S&ED are bilateral consultative mechanisms.

[23] While USTR is statutorily mandated to report on the status of trade barriers and market access, it is not required to report on the status of implementation of JCCT and S&ED commitments.

[24] The number of reports responding to specific requirements has changed over time. For example, until 2010, the administration met the requirement for the National Trade Estimate Report on Foreign Trade Barriers with one report. Since then it has responded with three reports (*Report on Sanitary and Phytosanitary Measures*, NTE, and *Report on Technical Barriers to Trade*). Additionally, the administration addressed a reporting requirement on greenhouse gas technologies with stand-alone reports in 2006 and 2007 and subsequently addressed the requirement with an appendix to the NTE report.

[25] Key agencies involved in this process include Commerce (including the Patent and Trademark Office), Treasury, State, and USDA. This interagency structure, called the Trade Policy Committee, led by USTR, has two subordinate bodies—the Trade Policy Review Group (a management-level committee) and the Trade Policy Staff Committee (a senior staff-level committee subordinate to the management-level committee). Numerous subcommittees under the Trade Policy Staff Committee have also been established to facilitate interagency coordination on a variety of trade issues. According to USTR, the Trade Policy Staff Committee's Subcommittee on China meets in order to evaluate and coordinate U.S. engagement of China in the trade context and includes representatives from Commerce, Treasury, State, and USDA.

[26] We reviewed reporting for commitments made in 2010 and 2011 at the JCCT and S&ED, as well as reporting for all software legalization commitments made from 2008 through 2011.

[27] USTR has reported that one of its priority concerns in China is problematic industrial policies and that the beneficiaries of these policies are certain state-owned enterprises.

[28] According to USTR, software legalization refers to the goal of controlling the unauthorized copying of large numbers of legally obtained software programs by government agencies and state-owned enterprises.

[29] The "S&ED commitments" in our analysis refer to trade and investment commitments China made at the S&ED and its predecessor, the Strategic Economic Dialogue (SED), which took place from 2006 through 2008.

[30] The other three pillars of the S&ED's economic track focus on macroeconomic cooperation, global economic governance, and financial markets. The United States and China discuss financial services trade issues under the financial markets pillar.

[31] GAO, *World Trade Organization: Analysis of China's Commitments to Other Members*, GAO-03-4 (Washington, D.C.: October 2002).

[32] According to USTR, the WTO standing committees meet regularly to allow members to exchange views, to work to resolve questions of compliance with commitments, and to work to improve the global trading system. The standing committees do not include negotiating bodies or dispute settlement panels.

In: China and the U.S.
Editor: Arthur Santoni

ISBN: 978-1-63321-156-8
© 2014 Nova Science Publishers, Inc.

Chapter 3

24TH U.S. - CHINA JOINT COMMISSION ON COMMERCE AND TRADE FACT SHEET[*]

United States Department of Commerce

INTRODUCTION

U.S. Commerce Secretary Penny Pritzker and U.S. Trade Representative Michael Froman, together with Chinese Vice Premier Wang Yang, co-chaired the 24th U.S.-China Joint Commission on Commerce and Trade (JCCT) in Beijing, China on December 19th – 20th, 2013. They were joined by U.S. Secretary of Agriculture Tom Vilsack to address agricultural concerns. Other participants included U.S. Ambassador to China Gary Locke, U.S. Trade and Development Agency Director Leocadia Zak, and representatives from the State and Treasury Departments.

The following outcomes were achieved.

Government Procurement

China will accelerate its negotiation on accession to the WTO Agreement on Government Procurement (GPA) and submit a revised offer in 2014 that is on the whole commensurate with the coverage of GPA parties.

---

[*] This is an edited, reformatted and augmented version of a fact sheet, dated December 20, 2013.

Intellectual Property Rights and Localization of IPR and Technology

Trade Secret Protection and Enforcement

As a priority item in its 2014 Action Plan, China's National Leading Group on Combating IPR Infringement and the Manufacture and Sales of Counterfeit and Substandard Goods commits to adopt and publish an Action Program on trade secrets protection and enforcement that is expected to include:

- Concrete enforcement actions;
- Improvements of public awareness about the importance of not infringing trade secrets and the penalties for infringement; and
- Requirements for strict compliance with all laws, regulations, rules and other measures on trade secrets protection and enforcement by all enterprises and individuals.

China will welcome U.S. suggestions for actions to be taken to implement the Leading Group's Action Program, and will provide the United States with updates as it implements the plan.

The United States and China commit to cooperate in 2014 on proposals to amend the trade secret law and on related legislative and policy issues. China shall give serious consideration to U.S. legislative reform proposals.

Data Disclosure Requirements for Pharmaceutical Patents

China re-affirms that the Chinese Patent Guidelines permit patent applicants to file additional data after filing their patent applications, and that the Guidelines are subject to Article 84 of the Law on Legislation to ensure that pharmaceutical inventions receive patent protection. China affirms that this interpretation is currently in effect for patent examinations, re-examinations, and representations before the Courts. Relevant Chinese and U.S. agencies will continue to engage on specific cases.

Legitimate Sales

The United States and China reaffirm their commitment to foster a better IP protection environment by combating IPR infringement and counterfeit goods, with the result of facilitating the sales of legitimate IP-intensive goods and services. The United States and China recognize the importance of this issue and will conduct further discussions in 2014, including exchanges of relevant information, on detailed approaches towards this goal.

Official Use Vehicles

China commits not to finalize or implement the 2012 Draft Party and Government Organ Official Use Vehicle Selection Catalogue or the 2011 Detailed Rules on the Administration of Optional Official Vehicle Catalogue for Party and Government Organs, which would have effectively excluded vehicles produced by foreign and foreign-invested enterprises from important procurement opportunities.

Procedural Improvements to Enhance Civil IP Enforcement

The United States and China commit to discuss and work towards improvements to their respective civil IP enforcement systems including through the JCCT IPR Working Group. The United States will raise issues including enhancements to the civil IP enforcement system, such as access to courts, improving discovery methods, enhancing evidence and asset preservation, and maintaining an accessible collection of decisions in IP cases.

Graphical User Interfaces

China has stepped up its efforts to advance innovation in the fast growing information and communications technologies sector by publishing draft Guidelines for public comment to extend design-patent protection to graphical user interfaces.

Regulatory Obstacles

ZUC Encryption Algorithm

China commits that in MIIT's testing and network access license approval processes for 4G devices, it will not require applicants to divulge source code or other sensitive business information in order to comply with ZUC provisions in the application process.

CCC Mark Testing and Certification

Building on commitments made at the 23rd JCCT, China reaffirms that for future designation of CCC testing and certification organizations, China's review of applications from foreign-invested entities registered in China will use the same conditions as are applicable to Chinese domestic entities. The specific implementation of this commitment will take place by Spring 2014.

Market Access for U.S. Beef

Both sides will strive for the resumption of U.S. beef access by July 2014 on the basis of mutually agreed conditions. Both sides will strive for effective solutions to common concerns regarding U.S. beef trade and promote U.S. beef exports to China.

Travel and Tourism Memorandum of Understanding

China and the United States agreed to expand the Memorandum of Understanding opening the market for the sale of packaged group leisure travel from China to the United States to include Gansu and Qinghai provinces.

COOPERATIVE ACTIVITIES

U.S.-China IP Cooperation and Technical Assistance

The U.S. Trade and Development Agency signed a Memorandum of Understanding (MOU) with the Chinese Ministry of Commerce under the U.S.-China IP Cooperation Framework Agreement (CFA) to provide a program of technical assistance to Chinese intellectual property agencies, courts and the legislature on strengthening the protection and enforcement of intellectual property rights, and on adopting and maintaining innovation policies that are non-discriminatory and pro-competitive. The program consists of four workshops and one two to three week U.S.-based training program, which complement three other workshops and two U.S. study visits of two to three weeks that the U.S. Patent and Trademark Office will also be supporting under the CFA.

Administrative Licensing

In Spring 2014, the United States and China will continue their joint exchange on administrative licensing rules to further enhance mutual understanding of the two sides' administrative licensing procedures and their impact on the business community. These discussions will include the U.S. and Chinese business communities and discuss administrative licensing including the challenges of administrative licensing decisions in both countries.

U.S.-China Legal Exchange

The U.S. Department of Commerce and China's Ministry of Commerce successfully led the 2013 U.S.-China Legal Exchange, during which Chinese government representatives informed members of the U.S. business, legal, and academic communities in Boston, Massachusetts, Washington, DC, and Orange County, California, of recent developments in specific areas of Chinese commercial law. To promote greater U.S.-China trade, the Chinese representatives described developments in the Chinese legal regimes governing entrepreneurship, and energy conservation and renewable energy. Both sides agreed to convene the 2014 Legal Exchange in China, and to work together promptly to agree on the topics of the exchange and the cities in China where it will take place.

Enforcement Against Counterfeit Semiconductors

The United States and China agree to continue dialogue on increasing enforcement against counterfeit and substandard semiconductors and enhancing interagency coordination to combat counterfeit and substandard semiconductors. The United States and China also agree to increase cooperation on cross-border investigations relating to counterfeit and substandard semiconductors case investigations.

Trademark – Bad Faith Trademark Registrations

The United States and China agree to continue communications and exchanges on the issue of bad faith trademark registrations through existing bilateral and plurilateral channels.

Chapter 4

U.S. FACT SHEET: ECONOMIC TRACK FIFTH MEETING OF THE U.S.-CHINA STRATEGIC AND ECONOMIC DIALOGUE[*]

United States Department of the Treasury

This week, Secretary Jacob J. Lew led discussions on our economic priorities with the Chinese delegation, headed by Vice Premier Wang Yang. They were joined by leaders from 17 U.S. government agencies, and heads and senior officials representing all key Chinese economic ministries. Through the Economic Track of the Strategic and Economic Dialogue (S&ED), the Obama Administration is working to deliver concrete benefits for U.S. firms and workers from our economic relationship with China. As the world's second largest economy, it is important that China act in accordance with international norms and rules and pursue a growth strategy that relies more on domestic demand and less on resource intensive exports. This week, we saw engagement through the S&ED Economic Track yield real progress in addressing investment barriers, leveling the playing field, and strengthening intellectual property protection.

Negotiating a High-Standard U.S.-China Bilateral Investment Treaty (BIT): China announced its intention to pursue a BIT with the United States that, for the first time, will cover all phases of investment, including market access, and sectors of the Chinese economy (except for any limited and

---

[*] This is an edited, reformatted and augmented version of a fact sheet, dated July 12, 2013.

transparent negotiated exceptions). A high standard U.S.-China BIT is a priority for the United States and is critical to leveling the playing field for American workers and businesses. A successful BIT negotiation would open up China's highly restrictive system to foreign investment and help create a wide range of opportunities for U.S. firms to participate in the Chinese market. We are pleased by China's interest in moving forward with negotiations that could address a range of U.S. commercial and economic priorities, including greater market access, removal of investment barriers, protections against technology transfer, and increased transparency.

Opening China's Services Market to U.S. Firms: China committed to open up further to foreign investment in services, including through the establishment of the Shanghai Free Trade Zone pilot. While detailed guidelines are forthcoming, the pilot is expected to permit foreign enterprises to compete on the same terms as Chinese firms across a wide range of services sectors. U.S. services firms are among the most competitive in the world and will contribute to China's services market as it grows and becomes more open to foreign investment. China also identified the e-commerce and commercial factoring sectors as areas for future liberalization to foreign investment. In addition, China plans to reduce the tax burden on services firms, by extending its VAT-for-Business pilot program to cover the entire country and to cover additional sectors in 2014.

Unlocking China's Procurement Market: China has not joined the WTO Government Procurement Agreement, despite having one of the world's largest and fastest growing procurement markets. China announced that it will take additional steps to open its market to U.S. firms by committing to submit a revised offer to the WTO Government Procurement Committee by the end of the year that will include improvements in some key areas such as lowered thresholds and increased coverage of sub-central entities. China also committed to begin intensive technical discussions with the United States this summer with the aim of tackling remaining obstacles to China's GPA accession.

Enhancing Cyber Security and Protecting Intellectual Property Rights (IPR): Innovation is fundamental to America's competitiveness and growth, and preventing the theft of U.S. intellectual property (IP), including trade secrets, remains a top Administration priority. During the S&ED, Chinese officials acknowledged U.S. concerns over the growing problem of the cyber-enabled theft of trade secrets and business confidential information. U.S. and Chinese economic officials discussed the need to address this issue head on. China pledged to better protect against trade secret misappropriation through strengthened enforcement. China also committed to take concrete measures to promote the use of legal software by its state-owned enterprises (SOEs), including state-owned financial institutions, which account for a major share of the country's economy and computer users.

Developing International Guidelines on Export Finance: To help ensure that U.S. exports are not disadvantaged by cheap Chinese government financing, China affirmed its support for the current multilateral negotiation of sectoral guidelines as concrete progress towards achieving our joint commitment to conclude negotiations in 2014 for new comprehensive international guidelines on export financing by the major providers of export credits that would be consistent with international best practices.

Fostering Energy Transparency, Collaboration, and Reform: China pledged to increase the transparency and quality of the information it publishes on its energy sector, which will help to smooth the functioning of global energy markets. China also pledged to cooperate with the United States on policies for managing its oil stocks.

Fostering Participation in China's Energy Sector: China committed to accelerate the development of the legal and regulatory framework in the unconventional oil and natural gas sectors, a move which will help China to realize the potential of its domestic energy resources. China also announced that it welcomes participation by U.S. companies in energy development.

Promoting Legal and Regulatory Transparency: After a several year hiatus, China pledged to re-engage in a regular transparency dialogue at the Vice Minister level, which will enhance our ability to ensure that U.S. firms doing business in China are provided greater legal and regulatory certainty.

Exchange Rate Liberalization: China committed to move to a market-determined exchange rate. This is a critical part of China's efforts to rebalance its economy, as it will both reorient Chinese production towards goods for domestic residents and strengthen the purchasing power of the growing Chinese middle class. Since June 2010, when China moved the renminbi off its peg against the dollar, the renminbi has appreciated by over 16 percent against the dollar after accounting for differences in inflation. Since 2005, the renminbi has appreciated by about 35 percent against the dollar. China pledged to continue taking steps to let the market play a fundamental role in exchange rate formation, and also indicated its active consideration of subscribing to the international standard for public reporting of reserves data, the IMF's Special Data Dissemination Standard (SDDS), which would be a significant step forward in enhancing its reserve transparency.

Strengthening Financial Regulatory Cooperation: China's securities regulator announced that it will begin providing certain audit work papers to the Securities and Exchange Commission and the Public Company Accounting Oversight Board, an important step towards resolving a long-standing impasse on enforcement cooperation related to companies that are listed in the United States. U.S. and Chinese audit regulators also committed to accelerating efforts towards establishing a cooperation mechanism for cross border audit oversight.

Expanding Opportunities for U.S. Financial Services Providers: China pledged to continue to open up its financial sector to U.S. participation. China pledged that locally-incorporated foreign banks and securities firms will be able to directly trade government bond futures, and to encourage investment by foreign and domestic institutional investors in these products. China also welcomed participation by foreign firms in corporate bond underwriting and pledged to facilitate further evaluations of interested underwriters for participation in this market. China pledged to expand its consumer finance company pilot program to new cities and to additional foreign and domestic firms, which will increase the availability of financial services to Chinese households and help boost consumption. As it continues to move forward with renminbi internationalization, China welcomed participation by foreign banks in renminbi settlement of cross-border trade and investment.

Developing China's Financial Markets: To help channel capital to the most productive investments, and away from less efficient SOEs, China pledged to expand the pricing flexibility of financial market participants, advance market-based interest rate reform, and let the market play a larger role in credit allocation. China announced plans to re-launch government bond futures, which will support interest rate liberalization by helping to establish a benchmark interest rate yield curve. In addition, China will boost income security for Chinese households and support capital markets development through a commitment to promote tax-deferred pensions on a pilot basis, which it will expand to new cities and provinces, and welcome foreign firms' participation.

Boosting Household Consumption: China is taking a number of additional steps to boost household income and purchasing power, enabling households to spend more on goods and services, including from U.S. suppliers. To reduce the need for precautionary household savings, which often end up being invested in China's export sector, China pledged to significantly increase social security and employment spending by two percentage points of total fiscal spending by the end of 2015.

Boosting SOE Dividend Payouts: China pledged to increase the dividends paid by its SOEs and to increase the SOE dividend revenue transferred to social welfare, rather than retaining earnings within the SOE sector. This will increase the resources available to support social welfare programs for households, while reducing the resources available to support SOEs.

Eliminating Preferential Input Pricing for SOEs: China for the first time pledged to ensure that enterprises of all forms of ownership have equal access to inputs, such as energy, land, and water, and to develop a market-based mechanism for determining the prices of those inputs. This will help level the playing field for domestic and foreign enterprises competing with Chinese SOEs that often pay below market cost for their inputs, and are key steps to ensuring that SOEs do not have an artificial advantage.

INDEX

A

abuse, 103
access, 27, 30, 42, 43, 48, 57, 68, 72, 82, 96, 115, 116, 120, 123
accountability, 88, 95
accounting, 104, 121
accreditation, 35
acquisitions, 24, 25, 26, 102
additives, 92
advancement, 38
aerospace, 35
affirming, 78, 81, 103
agencies, 41, 44, 59, 72, 73, 77, 83, 84, 85, 86, 92, 97, 98, 99, 102, 106, 107, 108, 110, 111, 114, 116, 119
agricultural exports, 46
agriculture, 65, 76, 81, 89, 91, 107
Alaska, 28
annual rate, 9
annual review, 41
antidumping, 3, 20, 48, 67, 105
arrest, 66
Asia, 15, 44, 67, 69, 73, 75, 109
assessment, 108
assets, 16, 17, 23, 24, 25, 26, 28, 33, 34, 53, 61
assimilation, 37
ATP, 12
audit(s), 75, 93, 109, 122

Austria, 66
authority, 67, 92
Automobile(s), 21, 64

B

ban, 83, 102
bank holding companies, 26
banking, 33, 34, 46
banks, 16, 26, 32, 34, 122
barriers, viii, 2, 20, 25, 29, 32, 46, 60, 61, 71, 73, 74, 75, 81, 83, 85, 86, 87, 88, 89, 90, 91, 93, 94, 95, 104, 107, 108, 109, 111, 119, 120
base, 63
batteries, 21
bauxite, 48
BEA, 16, 19, 20, 61, 62, 63
beef, 116
Beijing, viii, 24, 37, 38, 44, 57, 66, 69, 77, 98, 107, 113
Belgium, 9
benchmarks, 59, 92
beneficiaries, 111
benefits, 15, 36, 38, 55, 68, 77, 98, 119
beverages, 92
bilateral, v, 18, 19, 30, 71, 119
bilateral relationship, 77
bilateral trade relations, vii, 3
blame, 4

blueprint, 37
bond market, 58
bonds, 23
branching, 29
Brazil, 9
breakdown, 34
budget deficit, 16
businesses, 28, 33, 36, 37, 42, 43, 44, 62, 120

C

cabinet(s), 11, 55
cables, 86
Cambodia, 61
capital markets, 122
cash, 49
categorization, 72, 75, 80, 99, 107
Census, 12
certification, 104, 115
challenges, 2, 30, 43, 55, 59, 60, 73, 84, 93, 95, 117
Chamber of Commerce, 30, 36, 37, 40, 42, 51, 66, 67, 68
chemical(s), 8, 49, 61
Chicago, 26
chicken, 3
Chile, 69
Chinese firms, vii, 3, 20, 23, 24, 29, 32, 33, 36, 37, 40, 46, 47, 49, 51, 57, 58, 63, 67, 110, 120
Chinese government, 2, 3, 16, 23, 24, 27, 28, 29, 30, 32, 33, 34, 35, 36, 39, 41, 42, 43, 44, 47, 51, 52, 53, 54, 63, 64, 65, 67, 78, 98, 99, 108, 109, 117, 121
Chinese People's Liberation Army, 34, 45
Chinese Vice Premier Wang Yang, viii, 113
cities, 52, 117, 122
citizens, 49
City, 21, 26
clarity, 93
climate, 30, 55
climate change, 55
coal, 33
coke, 48

commerce, 91
commercial, vii, 1, 3, 10, 16, 19, 22, 24, 25, 34, 39, 42, 43, 44, 60, 61, 67, 74, 77, 84, 87, 94, 117, 120
commercial bank, 34
commercial ties, vii, 1, 3, 16, 19
commodity, 58
communication, 97
Communist Party, 3, 31
communities, 117
community, 117
compensation, 42
competition, 2, 29, 60, 90, 109
competitive advantage, 41, 49
competitiveness, 35, 38, 44, 120
competitors, 40
complement, 116
compliance, 32, 47, 48, 90, 104, 109, 111, 114
computer, 10, 13, 27, 28, 35, 44, 61, 121
computer use, 121
computing, 27
conference, 18
Congress, 1, 3, 4, 18, 26, 28, 43, 52, 53, 54, 55, 62, 64, 65, 67, 73, 88, 89, 90, 92, 93, 95, 108
congressional budget, 108
congressional hearings, 92
consensus, 107, 110
conservation, 49
Constitution, 92
construction, 21, 33
consumer goods, 58
consumers, vii, 1, 9, 33, 60, 87
consumption, 2, 9, 57, 59, 60, 122
controversial, 64
conversations, 75
cooperation, 23, 43, 56, 57, 59, 94, 100, 104, 105, 106, 109, 111, 117, 122
coordination, 35, 41, 78
copper, 22
copyright, 41, 110, 101
corporate sector, 32
cost, vii, 1, 2, 15, 19, 20, 32, 33, 38, 39, 42, 49, 53, 123

counterfeiting, 41
counterterrorism, 55
countervailing duty, 54, 103
country of origin, 20
covering, 4, 22, 29, 45
critical infrastructure, 25
culture, 55
currency, vii, 2, 3, 16, 31, 48, 52, 53, 54, 59, 62, 68
current account, 53
current account surplus, 53
customers, 20
Customs and Border Protection, 39, 66
cyber espionage, vii, 2, 3, 4, 26, 45
cyber-attack, 38
cyberspace, 4, 45

D

damages, 40
database, 98, 99
deficit, 5, 12
Department of Agriculture, 25, 76
Department of Commerce, v, 38, 73, 77, 98, 109, 113
Department of the Treasury, v, 73, 77, 109, 119
depository institutions, 61, 62
deposits, 57
depreciation, 62
deterrence, 18
developing countries, 91
dialogues, viii, 2, 55, 60, 71, 72, 73, 74, 75, 77, 78, 81, 82, 88, 95, 96, 97, 98, 99
diplomatic efforts, 91
direct investment, 16, 62
disappointment, 4
discrimination, 30, 48
diseases, 92
distribution, 46, 47, 50, 107
Doha, 46
domestic demand, 119
domestic laws, 102
draft, 65, 92, 96, 97, 101, 105, 115
drugs, 109

dumping, 21, 48, 60, 103

E

earnings, 123
East Asia, 26
e-commerce, 120
economic competitiveness, 25
economic cooperation, 56, 109
economic crisis, 56
economic development, 29, 32
economic downturn, 5
economic efficiency, 60
economic growth, vii, 3, 5, 7, 10, 31, 38, 54, 56, 59
economic institutions, 68
economic losses, 38, 39
economic power, 59
economic reform(s), 2, 3, 4, 7, 31, 32, 47, 60
economic relations, 1, 4, 23, 45, 119
education, 55
embassy, 69, 86, 107
emergency, 105
emigration, 61
employees, 28, 41, 61, 64
employment, 21, 23, 29, 39, 44, 59, 122
energy, 27, 28, 29, 55, 59, 65, 69, 94, 107, 117, 121, 123
energy conservation, 29, 117
enforcement, 2, 32, 39, 40, 41, 42, 46, 47, 50, 51, 57, 89, 90, 101, 114, 115, 116, 117, 121, 122
engineering, 15, 21, 38, 62
entrepreneurship, 117
environment(s), 30, 40, 49, 55, 65, 69, 76, 87, 114
Environmental Protection Agency, 76
environmental technology, 33
EPS, 48
equipment, 10, 11, 13, 21, 28, 35, 49, 62, 68
equities, 16, 23
equity, 25, 29, 58, 94
espionage, vii, 2, 3, 4, 26, 28, 44, 45, 66
Eurasia, 73

Europe, 44, 73
European Union, 48, 51, 68, 90
evidence, 47, 62, 75, 104, 109, 115
examinations, 114
exchange rate, 16, 52, 54, 121
exercise, 99
exhaustible natural resources, 49
expenditures, 35
export control, 68
export market, vii, 1, 5, 6, 7, 9, 75, 95
export subsidies, 46, 47, 49, 50, 54, 91, 103
exporters, 16, 53, 57, 68, 91
exports, vii, viii, 1, 5, 7, 8, 10, 12, 13, 25, 29, 31, 42, 53, 54, 57, 63, 68, 71, 72, 74, 87, 88, 90, 103, 107, 109, 111, 116, 119, 121

F

factories, 24
fairness, 106, 110
faith, 117
Fannie Mae, 16, 23
farms, 63
FDI, 16, 18, 19, 20, 22, 23, 24, 29, 31, 32, 47, 58, 59, 60, 61, 62, 63, 64
FDI inflow, 19, 29
federal agency, 19
federal government, 16, 52
Federal Register, 86
Federal Reserve, 26
feedstuffs, 92
fiber, 27
fiber optics, 27
filament, 8
films, 42, 50
financial, 2, 23, 33, 43, 46, 50, 51, 53, 55, 56, 57, 58, 59, 64, 104, 109, 111, 121, 122
financial firms, 57
financial markets, 58, 109, 111
financial sector, 57, 122
financial support, 2, 64
financial system, 56
food, 4, 25, 61, 63

Food and Drug Administration, 25
food safety, 4, 25, 63
food security, 25
footwear, 12
force, 27, 43
foreign affairs, 77
foreign banks, 122
foreign companies, 64
foreign direct investment, 16, 18, 29, 107
foreign exchange, 7, 23, 53, 62
foreign firms, vii, 3, 13, 30, 32, 34, 36, 37, 38, 41, 42, 46, 47, 50, 65, 107, 122
foreign investment, 31, 58, 63, 64, 68, 90, 102, 110, 120
foreign person, 24
foreign policy, 17
formation, 121
framing, 87
France, 9
Freddie Mac, 16, 23
free market economy, 2, 31
free trade, 2, 31, 60, 69
freedom, 61
funding, 49
funds, 19, 83

G

GAO, viii, 71, 72, 73, 75, 76, 80, 96, 97, 99, 100, 106, 111
GATT, 46
GDP, 9, 32, 33, 38, 61
General Agreement on Tariffs and Trade, 46, 90
General Motors, vii, 1, 10
Georgia, 21
Germany, 9
global demand, 53
global economy, 56, 68
global security, 44
global trade, 36
globalization, 13, 31, 64
goods and services, 7, 68, 106, 109, 114, 122
governance, 109, 111

Index

government procurement, 35, 36, 37, 51, 65, 68, 85, 89, 91, 100, 101, 107
government spending, 10
governments, 33, 37, 41, 52, 64, 74, 75, 77, 92, 93, 98, 102
GPA, 2, 31, 51, 52, 58, 60, 68, 73, 82, 83, 106, 110, 113, 120
grades, 27
grants, 26
greed, 101, 109, 116
greenhouse, 91, 94, 111
greenhouse gas, 91, 94, 111
gross domestic product, 32, 35, 38
growth, 6, 7, 9, 35, 41, 53, 56, 59, 61, 64, 119, 120
growth rate, 6
guidance, 32
guidelines, 59, 120, 121
Guinea, 61
Gulf of Mexico, 28

H

hacking, 41
health, 10, 47, 49, 55, 56, 57, 65, 92, 103
health care, 10
hiring, 24
history, 44
Hong Kong, 9, 13, 19, 34, 39, 61
host, 28
House, 24, 26, 44, 54, 67, 73, 74
House of Representatives, 73, 74
household income, 9, 58, 122
human, 55, 69, 92
human right(s), 55, 69

I

identification, 54
IMF, 121
import substitution, 38
imports, vii, 1, 5, 10, 11, 12, 13, 14, 15, 38, 42, 47, 48, 50, 60, 68, 74, 75, 103
improvements, 37, 41, 100, 109, 115, 120

income, 32, 122
indigenous innovation, 35, 36, 37, 38, 41, 57, 65, 101
individuals, 114
Indonesia, 61
industrial policies, vii, 2, 3, 29, 30, 31, 32, 34, 40, 54, 94, 111
industrial policy, 41, 93, 103
industries, 2, 4, 7, 10, 29, 30, 32, 33, 38, 39, 41, 42, 45, 49, 50, 53, 57, 62, 84, 87, 103, 110
industry, viii, 4, 22, 44, 45, 49, 51, 62, 64, 65, 71, 74, 84, 86, 92, 97, 107, 109
inflation, 62, 121
information exchange, 94, 109
information technology, 4, 13, 33, 107
infrastructure, 7, 10, 23, 24, 27, 51
inhibitor, 4, 45
initiation, 3
inspections, 84, 93
institutions, 16, 61
intellectual property, vii, 2, 3, 25, 26, 31, 35, 36, 38, 39, 40, 43, 44, 63, 66, 78, 81, 84, 86, 87, 89, 91, 94, 101, 108, 109, 110, 116, 119, 120
intellectual property rights, 2, 25, 31, 35, 63, 78, 81, 86, 89, 91, 95, 101, 109, 110, 116
intelligence, 44, 63
interagency coordination, 111, 117
interest rates, viii, 1, 34, 57
international competitiveness, 12
International Monetary Fund, 62
international standards, 104
internationalization, 122
intervention, 32
intrusions, 44, 67
inventions, 114
investments, 16, 20, 23, 24, 36, 110, 122
investors, 19, 23, 30, 58, 63, 75, 82, 94, 102, 110, 122
IPR, 2, 30, 31, 32, 36, 37, 38, 39, 40, 41, 42, 44, 46, 47, 50, 54, 57, 58, 59, 60, 114, 115, 120
issues, vii, viii, 3, 4, 25, 45, 47, 55, 56, 57, 66, 71, 74, 75, 77, 78, 81, 82, 84, 85, 86,

88, 89, 90, 91, 95, 97, 98, 102, 103, 104, 106, 107, 109, 111, 115

J

Japan, 9, 13, 17, 48, 61, 62, 68, 69, 75
Joint Commission on Commerce and Trade, v, viii, 36, 41, 65, 72, 73, 74, 79, 97, 113
joint ventures, 29, 41, 46, 58, 61
judicial interpretation, 78

K

Korea, 9

L

Laos, 61
law enforcement, 55
laws, 32, 41, 47, 50, 54, 57, 60, 101, 102, 105, 107, 109, 114
laws and regulations, 41, 47, 101, 105, 107
lead, 77, 92, 98
leadership, 59, 109
legal protection, 30
legislation, 52, 67, 92
leisure, 105, 116
liberalization, 47, 104, 120, 122
license fee, 39
life sciences, 35
lithium, 21, 25
loans, 32, 34, 49, 68
local government, 30, 32, 33, 35, 49, 56, 83, 106, 110
lower prices, 48, 58

M

machinery, 8, 61
magnesium, 48
major issues, 59
majority, 4, 19, 24, 33, 44, 63, 82
Malaysia, 61, 69

management, 33, 61, 62, 83, 104, 111
manganese, 48
manipulation, 53, 66
manufacturing, 13, 19, 21, 22, 25, 29, 34, 35, 41, 49, 53, 61, 62, 63, 64, 65
market access, 2, 32, 36, 38, 41, 42, 43, 50, 57, 58, 68, 82, 88, 93, 103, 106, 111, 119
market economy, 47, 57, 105
materials, 49, 110
measurement(s), 19
meat, 4, 8, 24
media, 3, 22, 26, 33, 61, 63
medical, 6, 8, 81, 86, 94, 107
membership, 46, 47
merchandise, 5, 10
mergers, 24, 26, 29, 102
metals, 33, 61
methodology, 75, 107
Mexico, 5, 9, 69
middle class, 5, 9, 121
migration, 61
military, 18, 28, 64
mineral resources, 65
mission, 45
Missouri, 25
misuse, 41
mobile phone, 10
modifications, 101
monopoly, 42, 107
multilateral, 102
multinational firms, 13
music, 42, 50

N

National Defense Authorization Act, 18
national security, 18, 24, 25, 26, 27, 28, 29, 63, 64, 102
natural gas, 121
natural resources, 49
negotiating, 111
negotiation, 30, 110, 111, 113, 120, 121
Netherlands, 9
networking, 28
neutral, 64, 106

Index

New Zealand, 61, 69
North America, viii, 8, 11, 71, 74
North Korea, 61

O

Obama, 3, 4, 25, 30, 45, 51, 63, 64, 119
Obama Administration, 3, 25, 30, 64, 119
obstacles, 120
OECD, 5, 29, 61, 64
officials, viii, 24, 25, 28, 29, 30, 38, 39, 46, 47, 51, 54, 55, 57, 58, 60, 62, 71, 72, 74, 75, 77, 78, 81, 82, 84, 85, 86, 87, 92, 95, 98, 107, 108, 109, 110, 119, 120
oil, 28, 33, 121
openness, 47, 102, 105
operations, 25
opportunities, 29, 30, 42, 44, 51, 57, 62, 74, 77, 105, 115, 120
organ, 34
Organization for Economic Cooperation and Development, 5
outreach, 72, 84
oversight, 122
ownership, 16, 23, 25, 29, 34, 36, 43, 46, 58, 61, 62, 64, 123
ownership structure, 34

P

Pacific, 2, 13, 14, 21, 60, 61, 73, 75, 109
participants, viii, 78, 85, 113, 122
patents, 101, 110
penalties, 114
permit, 109, 114, 120
perpetrators, 44
Peru, 69
pests, 92
pharmaceutical(s), 41, 81, 107, 114
Philippines, 61
phosphorus, 48
photonics, 28
piracy, 39, 40, 41, 42, 44, 85, 101
plants, 62, 103
playing, 49, 119, 120, 123
policy, 2, 3, 16, 17, 35, 44, 50, 53, 54, 73, 74, 78, 81, 87, 89, 92, 107, 114
policy issues, 114
policy makers, 2, 44, 73, 74
policymakers, 72, 87, 88, 95, 96, 97
political opposition, 28
politics, 63
pollution, 10, 29, 49
population, 7, 10, 65
poultry, 103
PRC, 43
precedent, 44
predictability, 106, 110
preferential treatment, 36
prejudice, 68
preparation, 84, 86, 92, 107, 109
preservation, 115
president, 45
President, 4, 23, 26, 36, 43, 45, 51, 55, 63, 65, 91, 92
President Obama, 4, 23, 26, 43, 45, 51, 55
pricing flexibility, 122
principles, 72, 78, 81, 83, 103
private enterprises, 42, 94
private firms, 34
private sector, 32, 44, 78, 85, 87, 92, 110
procurement, 22, 32, 35, 36, 37, 51, 52, 65, 68, 86, 100, 101, 104, 106, 110, 115, 120
producers, 21, 50, 51, 87, 104
production costs, 21
profit, 15
project, 21, 26
property rights, 72, 81, 89, 91, 92, 101
protection, 25, 31, 39, 41, 46, 56, 57, 58, 59, 60, 86, 91, 92, 101, 102, 106, 109, 110, 114, 115, 116, 119
protectionism, 30, 103
public awareness, 114
Public Company Accounting Oversight Board, 122
public debt, 17
public officials, 67
publishing, 105, 115
punishment, 17

purchasing power, 7, 121, 122

Q

quotas, 48, 68, 103

R

radio, 82
rare earth elements, 29
raw materials, 32, 48
reading, 108
recall, 86
recognition, 49
recovery, 56, 59
reform(s), vii, 3, 47, 54, 56, 57, 59, 94, 114, 121, 122
regulations, 30, 31, 32, 35, 36, 41, 47, 50, 65, 86, 102, 105, 109, 114
regulatory framework, 121
renewable energy, 35, 117
reputation, 4, 45
requirements, 30, 32, 42, 43, 46, 64, 65, 68, 88, 92, 96, 104, 111
research facilities, 28
researchers, 15
reserve currency, 62
reserves, 7, 23, 53, 62, 121
resistance, vii, 3
resolution, 30, 47, 49, 51
resources, 3, 23, 32, 39, 45, 65, 93, 121, 123
response, 30, 56, 84
restrictions, vii, 3, 29, 32, 47, 48, 50, 52, 53, 67, 68, 91, 103
restructuring, 33, 35
retail, 15, 107
retaliation, 42
revenue, 123
rewards, 49
rights, 46, 47, 50, 68, 89, 91, 95, 101, 106, 110
risk(s), 4, 18, 27, 45, 92
risk assessment, 18
rubber, 8

rule of law, 47
rules, 3, 32, 36, 46, 47, 48, 50, 51, 57, 67, 99, 102, 105, 106, 114, 117, 119
rules of origin, 106

S

safety, 10, 25, 47, 57, 62, 63, 94
sanctions, 2, 60
savings, 122
science, 35, 55
scope, 4, 45, 75, 89
Secretary of Agriculture, viii, 113
Secretary of Commerce, 44, 96
Secretary of Defense, 18, 62
Secretary of the Treasury, 25, 27, 56, 96
securities, viii, 1, 16, 17, 18, 23, 58, 62, 122
securities firms, 122
security, 4, 24, 25, 27, 28, 31, 44, 45, 64, 65, 102, 107, 122
SED, 55, 73, 74, 77, 98, 100, 103, 105, 106, 109, 111
seizure, 66
semiconductor(s), 11, 27, 51, 117
Senate, 25, 54, 63, 64
service industries, 65
services, 3, 7, 11, 22, 23, 47, 48, 50, 52, 57, 58, 61, 87, 89, 91, 100, 105, 106, 109, 110, 111, 120, 122
shareholders, 29
signs, 52
silicon, 27, 48
Singapore, 9, 61, 69
social security, 59, 122
social welfare, 123
software, 22, 39, 40, 41, 42, 58, 73, 81, 83, 85, 93, 102, 103, 104, 107, 108, 111, 121
software code, 40
solar cells, 21
South Korea, 61
soybeans, 57
special drawing rights, 62
specialists, 44
speech, 4, 45
spending, 10, 51, 59, 122

Index

Spring, 116, 117
stakeholders, 2, 24, 31, 39, 72, 84, 88, 92, 93, 97, 107
state(s), 2, 22, 21, 23, 24, 26, 27, 28, 29, 30, 32, 33, 34, 35, 37, 42, 45, 52, 56, 60, 64, 67, 83, 85, 94, 98, 100, 103, 104, 109, 111, 121
state-owned enterprises, 23, 30, 32, 45, 52, 83, 85, 94, 100, 103, 104, 111, 121
statistics, 13
statutes, 16
steel, 21, 27, 33, 48, 49, 50, 84, 107
stimulus, 10
stock, 19, 20, 34, 58, 62
strategic cooperation, 59
Strategic Economic Dialogue, 55, 73, 74, 111
structure, 34, 59, 72, 78, 81, 111
subscribers, 10
Subsidies, 90
subsidy, 49, 53, 54, 90
supervision, 103
supplier(s), 13, 32, 48, 50, 94, 106, 110, 122
supply chain, 5, 13, 15
survival, 42
Switzerland, 9
synthetic fiber, 8

T

Taiwan, 13, 61
takeover, 28
tangible benefits, 74
target, 53, 67
tariff, 38, 46, 50, 53, 67, 68, 103, 104
tax breaks, 32, 33, 68
tax incentive, 65
tax policy, 51
taxation, 58
taxes, 36, 48, 58
teams, 110
technical assistance, 116
technical comments, 96
technological progress, 38
technologies, 27, 28, 91, 94, 107, 111, 115

technology, 2, 3, 12, 22, 24, 25, 26, 29, 30, 32, 35, 36, 37, 39, 40, 42, 43, 44, 45, 46, 55, 58, 60, 64, 65, 67, 68, 69, 100, 120
technology transfer, 32, 36, 42, 43, 46, 58, 65, 67, 120
telecommunications, 22, 26, 33, 34, 82, 107
tension(s), 1, 2, 31, 63
territory, 110
terrorism, 106
testing, 104, 107, 115
textiles, 12, 107
Thailand, 61
theft, 2, 4, 30, 38, 39, 40, 41, 44, 45, 59, 60, 67, 120
Title I, 61
Title IV, 61
tobacco, 33
tourism, 107
toys, 11, 12
tracks, 55, 77, 85
trade agreement, 4, 75, 90, 91, 92
trade commitments, vii, viii, 3, 57, 71
trade deficit, vii, viii, 3, 5, 12, 53, 71, 74
trade disputes, vii, 3, 31
trade liberalization, vii, 3, 47
trade policy, 17, 91
Trade Policy Staff Committee, 92, 111
trade remedy, 20, 57, 60, 103, 105
trademarks, 101, 110
training, 116
transactions, 48, 53
transparency, 24, 30, 32, 47, 49, 57, 58, 81, 88, 91, 102, 105, 106, 110, 120, 121
transport, 29, 65
transportation, 15, 62, 107
Treasury, viii, 16, 27, 62, 64, 71, 72, 73, 76, 77, 82, 85, 86, 92, 96, 98, 107, 108, 111, 113
Treasury Secretary, 27, 64
treatment, 4, 34, 46, 49, 50, 51, 58, 59, 60, 68, 82, 94, 101, 102, 106, 110
turnover, 87

U

U.S. Commerce Secretary Penny Pritzker, viii, 113
U.S. Department of Agriculture, 73
U.S. Department of Commerce, 65, 66, 117
U.S. Department of the Treasury, 18, 63, 64, 65
U.S. economy, 2, 5, 17, 24, 39, 54, 63, 64, 74
U.S. Export-Import Bank, 57
U.S. firms, vii, 1, 2, 5, 15, 21, 22, 30, 31, 38, 39, 41, 42, 43, 44, 51, 58, 64, 67, 75, 119, 120, 121
U.S. policy, 2, 5, 23, 24, 25, 30, 37, 47, 53
U.S. Secretary of Commerce, 77, 109
U.S. Trade Representative Michael Froman, viii, 113
U.S. Treasury, viii, 1, 16, 17, 18, 23, 42, 55, 62, 68, 77
UK, 9
underwriting, 122
urban, 7, 33, 65
urban areas, 7
urbanization, 65
USA, 22, 26
USDA, 73, 76, 96, 98, 107, 108, 111

V

VAT, 51, 106, 120
vehicles, 5, 8, 10, 61, 94, 107, 115
vested interests, 60
Vice President, 23, 42, 43
victims, 44
Vietnam, 61, 69
vote, 54
voting, 16, 26, 62

W

wages, 64
waiver, 44
war, 18
Washington, 4, 55, 57, 58, 62, 77, 86, 98, 111, 117
waste, 5
water, 59, 65, 123
wealth, 23, 83
weapons, 29
web, 101
websites, 84
welfare, 123
well-being, 56
White House, 23, 43, 63, 65, 67
White Paper, 65
wholesale, 61
wind farm, 26
wind power, 49, 107
wind turbines, 40
wood, 50
workers, 15, 19, 21, 23, 24, 30, 34, 38, 49, 61, 63, 64, 77, 98, 119, 120
working groups, 72, 76, 77, 84
World Trade Organization, vii, 2, 3, 31, 46, 65, 67, 73, 74, 100, 107, 111
worldwide, 13, 36, 62, 89, 103
worry, 62
WTO obligations, vii, 3, 50

Y

yield, 119, 122
yuan, 52, 68

Z

zinc, 48